TO THE
LIGHTHOUSE

Peter Johnson and John Walls

photography by **Richard Paddle**

TO THE

VICTORIA · VANCOUVER · CALGARY

LIGHTHOUSE

An Explorer's Guide to the **ISLAND LIGHTHOUSES**
of **SOUTHWESTERN BC**

Heritage House Publishing Company Ltd.
heritagehouse.ca

CATALOGUING INFORMATION AVAILABLE FROM LIBRARY AND ARCHIVES CANADA

978-1-77203-046-4 (pbk)
978-1-77203-047-1 (epub)
978-1-77203-048-8 (epdf)

Edited by Lara Kordic
Proofread by Grace Yaginuma
Cover and book design by Jacqui Thomas
Cover photos by John Walls (*front*) and Richard Paddle (*back*)
Interior photos by Richard Paddle unless otherwise indicated.

The interior of this book was produced on 100% post-consumer recycled paper,
processed chlorine free, and printed with vegetable-based inks.

Heritage House acknowledges the financial support for its publishing program
from the Government of Canada through the Canada Book Fund (CBF), Canada
Council for the Arts, and the Province of British Columbia through the British
Columbia Arts Council and the Book Publishing Tax Credit.

19 18 17 16 15 1 2 3 4 5

Printed in Canada

Foreword ... **8**

How to Use This Book ... **10**

Introduction: Towards the Light ... **13**

TWENTY-FIVE ISLAND LIGHTHOUSES OF SOUTHWESTERN BC ... 31

GREATER VICTORIA

1   Sheringham Point   **33**

2   Race Rocks   **42**

3   Fisgard   **50**

4   Trial Islands   **57**

5   Discovery Island   **65**

6   Fiddle Reef   **72**

GULF ISLANDS

7   East Point   **78**

8   Active Pass   **85**

9   Portlock Point   **93**

10   Porlier Pass   **100**

SALISH SEA

11   Entrance Island   **106**

12   Ballenas Islands   **112**

13   Sisters Islets   **118**

14   Chrome Island   **124**

15   Cape Mudge   **131**

WEST COAST OF VANCOUVER ISLAND

16 Carmanah Point   137

17 Pachena Point   144

18 Cape Beale   151

19 Amphitrite Point   158

20 Lennard Island   164

21 Estevan Point   171

22 Nootka   178

NORTH VANCOUVER ISLAND

23 Pulteney Point   185

24 Quatsino   192

25 Cape Scott   199

Glossary ... **206**

Appendix ... **210**

Acknowledgements ... **211**

Notes ... **212**

Index ... **217**

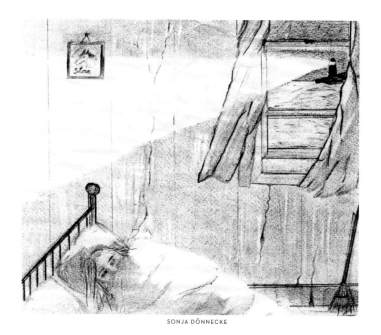

SONJA DÖNNECKE

NIGHT AFTER NIGHT, *summer and winter, the torment of storms . . . held their court without interference. Listening . . . from the upper rooms of the empty house only gigantic chaos streaked with lightning could have been heard tumbling and tossing, as the wind and waves disported themselves like the enormous bulks of leviathans whose brows are pierced by no light of reason, and mounted one on top of another, and lunged and plunged in the darkness or the daylight . . . in idiot games, until it seemed as if the universe were battling and tumbling, in brute confusion and wanton lust aimlessly by itself . . .*

Only the lighthouse beam entered the rooms for a moment, sent its sudden stare over bed and wall in the darkness of winter, looked with equanimity at the thistle and the swallow, the rat and the straw . . . a silvery, misty-looking tower with a yellow eye that opened suddenly, and softly, in the evening.

—VIRGINIA WOOLF, *To the Lighthouse,* 1927

FOREWORD

For me, the lighthouse and its keeper are a highly symbolic combo, both standing tall against elements that threaten to overwhelm and destroy, their only weapons a beam of light or the blast of a foghorn to warn of danger. The keeper, whose well-being depends on reserves of courage, stamina, and self-control in the face of extremes of solitude and weather, always reminds me of the stories of Paul Revere or Horatio on the bridge, patriots whose selfless and heroic acts held back or diverted forces that might have overwhelmed and destroyed the collective.

The fact that Revere was also an artist, a silversmith, appeals to me as well. The artist, as that great writer-mariner Joseph Conrad said, is involved in rescue work, rescuing the vanishing fragments of memory and giving them the permanence of art. In that sense, writers have a lot in common with the keepers of lighthouses, needing to be constantly alert to societal dangers, keeping themselves and the language in good shape and in readiness to meet social, political, and psychological challenges that are daily features of the human condition. The writer's task has been described as purifying the dialect of the tribe. I'm not enthusiastic about the word "purifying," as I like the idea of being adaptable to change. I prefer the notion of writing as a DEW, a distant early warning signal.

So, I salute author Peter Johnson, project manager John Walls, and photographer Richard Paddle for taking on this task of rescue work, protecting these historic symbols and landmarks, and keeping alive the intimate, heartwarming, and at times heartbreaking stories of the heroic light keepers and their families. If you imagine yourself at the helm of a ship, responsible for lives and desperately needed supplies, in dense fog or fighting gale-force winds off what has been aptly called the Graveyard of the Pacific, is there anyone you'd rather have on your side? I doubt it.

Their book, to use that other rich connotation, is a genuine keeper.

—**GARY GEDDES**,

winner of the Lieutenant Governor's Award
for Literary Excellence, author of *Sailing Home*
and *What Does a House Want?*

HOW TO USE THIS BOOK

To the Lighthouse explores some of the most striking examples of maritime architecture on the islands of southwestern British Columbia. With hundreds of fjords and inlets, the BC coast is thousands of kilometres long and almost unparalleled in grandeur. Yet this compelling geography with its labyrinthine waterways can be deceptively dangerous. Lighthouses—along with their dedicated and often-underappreciated keepers—have saved countless lives and prevented numerous tragedies.

Some of BC's historical lighthouses are gone now, but many remain. Lighthouse preservation societies are working to counter the neglect these stations suffered in the 1980s and 1990s, when many lighthouse keepers lost their jobs because of government cuts. Thanks to these organizations, some of BC's most treasured light stations remain manned. Some have become part of ecological reserves, and others have been designated as historically significant. In recognition of the efforts, in particular, of the Sheringham Point Lighthouse Preservation Society, 25 percent of the royalties from this book will go to this worthy organization.

Each of the lighthouses mentioned in this guide played a unique role in the history of BC. This province's very sovereignty, immigration, and industrial growth were touched by their presence and shaped by their roles. The adventures involved in searching out some of these structures today will not only open your eyes to their stories, but it will also take you to coves, bays, sounds, harbours, and seafoamed headlands so beautiful you will wonder how you missed seeing them for so long.

This is a guide for visitors who are tired of the typical tourist experience. Although a few of the twenty-five lighthouses presented in this book are within sight of a city or town and readily explored in a long afternoon, most require an easy, all-day adventure from a starting point of the BC capital of Victoria. A few demand a longer trek or a paddle deep into the wilderness. Each lighthouse is rated on a scale of accessibility ranging from ❶ (Dead Easy) to ❺ (Really, Really Hard):

❶ **Dead Easy** There's a parking lot, bike route, or transit stop nearby. This trip is easily done in an afternoon.

❷ **Still Easy** You'll probably have to take a Gulf Islands or north-island ferry and a short drive or bike ride to get there. This is a day's outing.

❸ **Moderate** Getting here requires a longer day hike, or a kayak, motorboat, or charter boat. It's a long, full-day trip.

❹ **Hard** Getting here requires a transit across open water, and/or a long hike. For most, it's an overnight trip.

❺ **Really, Really Hard** This trip is for experienced hikers, campers, and/or kayakers. Plan on being out for several days.

To the Lighthouse is a hands-on guide, something that ought to be jam-stained and dog-eared, with scribbled margins, crammed into a packsack, pannier, or glove compartment. Yet, it's also an armchair traveller's guide to lighthouse lore. While it does draw on interviews with light keepers and their children, as well as new historical information on the origins of lighthouse and place names, this book is indebted to writers that have gone before. There are more detailed books on BC lighthouses. We recommend the late Donald Graham's two volumes: *Keepers of the Light* and *Lights of the Inside Passage*. Graham's compassionate accounts of our early light keepers make for a fine winter read. Chris Jaksa and Lynn Tanod's *Guiding Lights* will dazzle you completely with contemporary interviews and fine photography.

What better way to spend an island vacation—or even just a weekend afternoon—than to seek out a windswept lighthouse standing firm on a headland overlooking the still-pristine coastal waters. The stories of these lighthouses are the stories of this coastal region; they remain magnificent shrines to a collective past, obelisks to our marine heritage.

INTRODUCTION:
TOWARDS THE LIGHT

THE MYTH

Perhaps, at the very beginning, it was idyllic. At first glance, there wasn't much to do, really. Just light the lamp in the evening, then blow it out in the morning. Beyond that, you did a bit of house painting here and there, kept some sort of a logbook now and then, and, from your perch on an arrestingly beautiful headland that overlooked the briny deep, you occasionally scanned the blue-grey and somnolent seas that prescribed your domain.

Alexander Dingwall and his family rowing home to their station on Green Island, circa 1916. Eve Dingwall would often tie her young children to the clothesline to keep fierce winds from blowing them off the rock into the sea. CITY OF VANCOUVER ARCHIVES

The rest of the time you could sit, or recline, beneath your soaring tower with a Scotch in one hand and a good book in the other. Or, being of a philosophical or poetic nature, you might even consider the long migrations of the offshore whales, or the calamitous gulls and bald eagles delighting in the updrafts far above. You might even write a few lyrics or play your guitar, all the while marvelling at your incredible good fortune in the solitude, independence, and unbounded tranquility amidst some of the most beguiling scenery in the world.

Hell, who needed much pay for such a job? Oh, and er . . . could you pass me my sunglasses, and perhaps add just a wee touch of water to my drink? It releases the flavour.

That's the myth.

THE REALITY

Part of this myth is true, but only a small part. The reality was different. The wages were meagre. The sun did shine—one or two days a year, in summer—but most days were foggy, and that was one of the reasons you were there. The other days, it rained. Hunger was not uncommon, especially if the supply ship didn't make its scheduled landing because of the continual storms. At times like this, before the telegraph or radio-telephone, solitude could easily become pathological. Deprived of family, someone sympathetic to talk to, another human being with whom to share the isolation, the aloneness was overwhelming. Bottled rage or alcoholism descended like the unending deluge.

Then, there was winter. The persistent lows made the lamp burn poorly, and its thick, black soot readily darkened the glass, the mirrors, and the prisms, every night. Cleaning it all wasn't easy; often the soot flaked and drifted down the tower and covered

Sheringham Point during its golden age. Note the third-order lamp in the cupola. CITY OF VANCOUVER ARCHIVES

the table where you ate and lived. When the drums of coal oil didn't arrive on time, you sat in darkness by your bedside lamp, giving favour to the all-important revolving beam or to the diesel engines, whose compressors must have air for the foghorn's lament. If the horns quit their groaning, you hand-worked them in the wet and hoped against hope that all was well out there, fearing to think what an offshore light might mean. As you ran low on coal, gale after gale blew through the chinks and crevasses of your damp little dwelling. Sickness lurked . . . pneumonia. An accident in these conditions you refused even to contemplate.

Adding a wife and kids to this equation might make things better, but they, too, would suffer the isolation. Children needed educating and socializing. Then, there were the warnings of bear and cougar in the woods, the fear of broken limbs on the rocks, and—horror of horrors—the risk of drowning while playing, unseen in the boiling surf.

▲ *Lightship No. 16, the old sealing schooner* Thomas F. Bayard *guided ships to New Westminster up the Fraser River from 1913 to 1956.* CITY OF VANCOUVER ARCHIVES

Then, when all Nature wreaked havoc upon the last of your humanity and there *was* a wreck, the best you could do was to watch other people's children, or their parents, drown—shipwrecked in the bedlam of the surf just yards from shore. If fate gave you a reprieve, you cast your own life to the wind, braved the tempest, and did what you could to save a few dumbfounded and innocent lives caught in a maelstrom beyond their understanding. You swore you would quit and move far inland . . . but you never did.

There was a dignity and an essence to this kind of life. You were a guardian, not of money or status but of others, unknown strangers who passed by safely in the night because of you. You were their keeper, their light keeper, one of those who tried to keep the existential darkness just beyond the horizon.

The main reason lighthouses remain so significant, quite apart from their role and unrivalled beauty on some of our most menacing headlands, lies in their unique position in history. They are firmly attached to the last great romantic days of sail, when mental fortitude and physical competence held sway. But they also unshakably straddle the less heroic, less graceful electronic age of great precision, lightning-fast computers, and automation. The tenure of the lighthouses, from their golden age in the nineteenth century, easily surpassed one hundred years.

From 1860 onwards, and for a century thereafter, lighthouses witnessed an absolute shift in the culture of the high seas. The composite-built, full-rigged ships such as the *John Bright* or the old *Gantock Rock* had already reached their perfection in the 1870s. They were superseded in the 1880s by iron clipper ships such as the *Cairnsmore*, flush-decked and narrow, racing from Land's End to Mumbai in just sixty days. When we see the last of these tall ships today on one of their crowded summer junkets, we see them in our mind's eye not in a group on a wharf, but alone on the high seas rolling down to St. Helena with staysails and gaff topsail flying, boisterous and beaming atop the glistening seas.

Rudyard Kipling was right:

> There be triple ways to take, of the eagle or the snake,
> Or the way of a man with a maid;
> But the sweetest way to me is a ship's upon the sea,
> In the heel of the North-East Trade.[1]

But the windjammers such as the *Cairnsmore, Thermopylae,* and the *Cutty Sark* were more than beautiful; they had to earn their keep. As Basil Lubbock wrote, they were built in the "last desperate fight put up by the sailing-ship owners against the attack of the cheaply run, jerry-built, over-insured tramp steamer."[2] The windjammers would last only ten years. The tramp steamers such as the SS *Talthybius* won the day. And in their time they, too, were eclipsed by ore carriers, bulk carriers, and giant container ships with unheard-of electronic sophistication that we see today in Vancouver's Burrard Inlet and English Bay and Tsawwassen's Delta Port.

The lighthouses witnessed all of this. Yet even technology and progress can't void human error. Rocks, reefs, and underwater ridges still remain. The 2006 sinking of the BC Ferries *Queen of the North* is a case in point. So, as the block-and-tackle mechanics of another age advanced from the mainsheet to the wheelhouse lever of the engine room telegraph, from semaphore-signal flags to the glowing blue monitors of differential GPS systems, the lighthouses were there. They focused light on one of the most active periods of change in Western civilization, and throughout all that time, more than any church spire, they stood for the simple, noble fact that we must look after each other.

They are beacons across time certainly, but they stand not just as monuments to our humanity, but as striking obelisks to the

▲ *Hand-operated foghorn on Entrance Island, circa 1930.* CITY OF VANCOUVER ARCHIVES

advancement of Science. It is within the context of this remarkable nineteenth-century scientific endeavour that the stories of the lighthouses and our exploration of them on this magical coast must begin.

A LOUSY DINNER, A GUILLOTINE, A GENIUS, AND A TREASURED ISLAND

They've been around for a while. The Egyptians had one at the mouth of the Nile. The Romans had one in Dover. Venice saw its first in 1312, and Antonio Columbus (Christopher's uncle) kept the light in Genoa in 1468.

Lighthouses, blazing out across the water also shine across time. Seeing them up close, or from the deck of a passing ferry, triggers something magic in us, even now. Patently bold, they stand doubly symbolic between our resolve to seek more, to wayfare beyond known horizons. Yet they stand, too, for the call home, the expression of a warm hearth and the hope of a refuge safe from those elemental forces outside the limits of our control.

The problem has really never changed. How big must a light be to be seen for kilometres out at sea? A lighted candle inside a glass might be seen two hundred metres, while early bonfires fretted and often burned their towers down to the ground. That's when the thinking began in earnest. Instead of using a single waxed string, why not put a series of strings together in a row? That invention was called a wick. But wax was expensive and burned fast, so whale oil or coal oil replaced it, causing the fuel to wick itself up to a brighter flame. More wick, more flame. Enclose the "lamp" in glass to protect it from the elements, put it up high enough, et voilà, a proper lighthouse!

Not so fast. The issue was the wick; its flat, thin shape still didn't cast enough light. The inherent weakness was the soot. More wick, more soot. Even ten wicked lamps stacked together still didn't produce a flame big enough to be seen thirty kilometres out to sea. Besides, the soot would have to be scraped daily from the glass housing, discounting the fact that the heat alone would shatter its glass completely. Besides, the space at the top of a lighthouse tower was usually quite limited, which compounded the problem of housing a light far more intense than could be emitted from a candle or a wick. Jamming in more wicked lamps didn't work, though for a time that was tried. The answer lay in improving the very nature of the beam. Clear-sighted eighteenth-century rationalism saved the day. The lighthouse lamp had to be bright for two reasons: to give a warning and to prompt a revelation.

Under full sail at ten knots, or under power at eighteen, ships approach land surprisingly quickly. A lighthouse must cast its beam far out to sea in all kinds of weather to give a mariner ample notice that his vessel is rapidly nearing an unknown shore.

Changing sails, taking soundings, readying to come about, and posting crews into the rigging to keep watch all took time as a reef, a rock, or underwater ledge lay ahead, poised and waiting like a cougar. Now increasingly anxious, the master mariner must begin an exacting protocol to ascertain, even as the wind and seas raged, just where exactly his ship was, in this booming, blasphemous negation.

Luckily, that same light also revealed to a competent skipper the real position of his vessel at sea. First, he must take a compass bearing on the light that glimmered ahead. Then he must draw that bearing as a line on his chart, which he labelled LOP, a line of position. The anxious captain then knew that his ship was somewhere along that line. Then, even as he charged through the darkness, he must not alter the course of his ship. He must now find another lighthouse or another headland and take yet another bearing, then plot that second LOP on the same chart. Where the two LOPs intersected, the mariner drew a small circle. That circle was a fix. If he was lucky, he might plot a third line of position and mark it on his chart. The circle then became known as a "cocked hat." His ship was within that circle. The captain had fixed his position. A first mate would confirm his master's bearings and note the lights and promontories that lay ahead. Then and only then, if it was necessary, could the watchful skipper order a course change, keeping his vessel, his cargo, his passengers, and crew out of harm's way. Without lights that penetrated far out to sea, and without charts, certain death stared them in the face.

Achieving that long-reaching light took daring, ingenuity and time. It began with mirrors, which had also been around for a quite a while. The Anatolians had polished black, volcanic obsidian into reflective mirrors five thousand years ago. The nervy idea of somehow bonding silvered metal to a hot sheet of glass is a bit more recent. Pre-Christian Lebanese alchemists discovered that pouring hot mercury over a still-glowing bubble of glass caused the mercury to adhere instantly to the outside of the bubble. When broken, the inside of the bubble formed perfectly silvered, concave mirrors. Yet, even a concave mirror allowed light to escape because of divergence—the property of light to diffuse in all directions. A lighthouse lamp required a special kind of mirror, one that shot out its reflected light all in the same direction.

It was the Swedish mathematician Jonas Norberg who, by 1757, knew that a parabola overcame divergence. So Norberg placed a wicked lamp at the focus point of a parabolic mirror and found that most of its light rays were reflected outwards horizontally. Norberg's improved lighthouse lamp with its parabolic mirror threw a beam visible, some said, for thirteen kilometres. The goal of a lamp with a range of fifty kilometres was fast approaching.

A LOUSY DINNER In 1789, the Swiss-French chemist François Argand was dining in a dimly lit Parisian restaurant when he dropped a decanter of good wine. *Tabernac!* He picked up a piece of its narrow glass neck and held it over the flame of the oil lamp at his table. Suddenly the flame burst into a light more intense than ever, and, more interestingly, it produced little soot. Argand went home and designed a new lamp, one with a metal, holed, tubular burner, which held a circular wick. Air boosted the flame like in no other lamp produced before. Then Argand paired his new lamp with a parabolic mirror. Suddenly, the light shone out with ten times the candle power of previous wicked lamps. To cut down on the soot, the inspired chemist used whale oil to feed this remarkable new flame. That was good. Then he packed several lamps together into one giant array. For a time the Argand lamp, with its reflective mirror and an array of wicked burners, became the lighthouse standard. Argand toyed with the idea of placing a convex lens in front of the array, but its mass overcrowded the space and constricted the airflow, causing soot to once again raise its ugly head. Besides, the whole damned assembly soon weighed upwards of twenty tons, and the use of whale oil would contribute to the massive decline of these leviathans of the deep.

A GUILLOTINE If you studied high school chemistry, you'll remember phlogiston like you remember acne. In 1770, most chemists believed that anything that burned contained particles called phlogiston (from the Greek word for "inflammable"). They theorized that the phlogiston was used up in the burning process, because when substances burned they lost weight. For example, remaining powdered-charcoal ash weighs less after burning than an unburned charcoal briquette. Phlogiston theory further postulated that air had a threshold level for the amount of phlogiston it could hold. When the phlogiston was used up, or the air became saturated, the fire went out.

Antoine Lavoisier was a maverick. He never believed the phlogiston theory because he found that some metals (such as phosphorus) actually gained weight when burned. Lavoisier weighed both the residue *and* the escaped gases. He theorized that the oxidation process simply lost particles to something else rather than disappearing altogether. By 1780, Lavoisier had had invented special fire lenses and adapted parabolic mirrors powerful enough to burn diamonds into both carbon and carbon dioxide. Again he weighed both, and the scales showed a gain. By 1789, Lavoisier's theory of oxidation and the law of the conservation of matter not only doomed the phlogiston theory, but it changed chemistry forever. Unfortunately, Jean-Paul Marat, a revolutionary, considered Lavoisier a threat to the French Revolution because he was both an aristocrat and an experimenter and had him guillotined on July 14, 1789 (Bastille Day). Fortunately, one of Lavoisier's students was a very bright lad indeed.

A GENIUS Even at sixteen, Augustin Fresnel's passion was lenses. As a child he knew that a magnifying glass readily ignited a piece of paper on a sunny day. As a teenager, after seeing a rainbow of light on the edge of a windowpane, he understood that prisms not only refracted light; they also intensified it. He knew, too, that large lenses and mirrors were very heavy. So in 1828, he constructed a small glass lens (a bulls-eye lens), around which he assembled hundreds of wafer-thin prisms, each projecting out from the one below. Each "ring" therefore became the edge of a larger, refractive mirror. These prismatic wafers captured nine-tenths of the light given off by any single, wicked oil lamp.

Suddenly there was unheard-of brilliance. Fresnel found that a mantle fed on gaseous acetylene instead of an oily wick increased his lamp's range to over fifty kilometres. The barrier had been broken, and although Fresnel's assemblies were still heavy, they worked. Brightness was based on an ordered scale—1 was brightest and largest and was called first order, while 7 was the dimmest and smallest and was dubbed seventh order. By 1850, the Chance Brothers of Birmingham, England, had become world renowned in the construction of the Fresnel prismatic reflectors, bulls-eye lenses, and the polished-brass housings that kept it all together. Fresnel didn't; he died of TB at age thirty-nine.

A TREASURED ISLAND The lighthouse builders on the BC coast learned their craft from the Europeans. They understood that only the great, interlocked granite slabs of the Kéréon Lighthouse off the rock-strewn coast of Brittany could withstand the waves of the North Atlantic. They saw the necessity of the first-order beacon in the Cape Agulhas Lighthouse, which guided ships around the southern coast of Africa. They copied lighthouses with their towers rising directly from the roofs of the keeper's dwelling, as in the Ponta das Contendas Lighthouse on the Azores. And they knew that the rotating lamp of the Fastnet Lighthouse stood out more clearly in its interval flash, warning ships away from the treacherous seas of the southwestern coast of Ireland.

But it was the Scots in the 1850s that inspired BC lighthouse builders the most—specifically, the builders of the lights at Barra Head and Skerryvore marking the Minch, that menacing body of water separating the Outer Hebrides from mainland Scotland. Robert Stevenson was an architect; by 1820 he was head of the Scottish Lighthouse Board. His sons, Alan, David, and Thomas, also became lighthouse engineers and had a hand in the construction of Barra Head. Thomas Stevenson hoped his own child would join the family dynasty. At nineteen, he accompanied his father on an inspection tour of lighthouses in Orkney and the Shetlands. The lad wrote, "Here we landed making a leap between the swells to the ridge and up a flight of steps 200 feet to the lighthouse of Muckle Flugga."[3] Thomas also told his son Robert about the lives of the local labourers who built and maintained these magnificent towers. One especially important life was that of John Silver, a tall young stonemason from Arisaig who helped build Barra Head, the highest lighthouse in all of Scotland.

The boy loved his father's tales of shipwrecks on the bleak, wet islands of the Outer Hebrides. But he became even more transfixed when his uncle Alan and grandfather Robert added other yarns of English revenue men, smugglers, and pieces of eight buried on Fidra, Mingulay, South Uist, and the Isle of Lewis.

The spellbound boy didn't become a lighthouse engineer like his forebears. He simply continued to tell stories. John Silver evolved into Long John Silver. And a map of Fidra he drew for his own child became immortalized in his most cherished tale,

Treasure Island. For Robert Louis Stevenson, lighthouses were his muse.

THE LIVES OF THE WICKIES

In the early days, light keepers used to call themselves wickies because their whole working lives revolved around the wick—tending the light. They couldn't go down for a bite of supper after the lamps were lit and the rotation apparatus that revolved around them were wound and set in motion. They had to remain in the lamp room at the top of the tower for at least an hour afterwards, making sure the wicks burned evenly and the giant clockwork contraption that slowly pirouetted the lot didn't break a critical tooth in one of its cogs.

At the time BC joined Confederation (1871), the Canadian government didn't tell would-be light keepers much, nor did they seem to ask much. If you could fog a mirror, you got the job. Two years before British Columbia joined Confederation, the federal Department of Marine and Fisheries issued a set of requirements for the admission of light keepers into the federal service. A candidate had to submit proof that he had only one job-related attribute: a certificate of ability to work and properly manage an open boat.

Beyond that, the requirements were the same as those of any other position aimed at male labourers between the ages of eighteen and fifty. Candidates had to present:

- a certificate of birth or other evidence of age.
- a certificate from a Medical Man as to [the candidate's] present state of health.
- a certificate from a schoolmaster or clergyman of being able to read and write, and of having a fair knowledge of Arithmetic.
- a certificate of former employment or Trade; if married or single; and if any family.

▲ *Diesel air compressor for the diaphones at Estevan Point, circa 1950.*

- a certificate of character from a former employer, including a clergyman or teacher.[4]

In the 1860s, only two lighthouses existed on the British Columbia coast—Fisgard and Race Rocks—and competition for the job was fierce. By 1912, over twenty lighthouses had been built, and that changed everything. That same year the Department of Marine issued an updated set of regulations for light keepers that required a separate thirty-nine-page booklet detailing over a hundred instructions.[5] By then, being a lighthouse keeper was a twenty-four-hour-a-day job.

THE DUTIES OF A LIGHT KEEPER

During the day, a light keeper had to:

❶ Extinguish and curtain the inside of the cupola as sunlight tarnished the prisms and mirrors. On the outside, on the gallery, he had to pick off the fish, dead birds, and droppings from the glass. Then he had to wipe the windows as required and trim all the wicks.

❷ Clean all the soot from the lamp burners, lenses, reflectors, and prisms.

❸ Twice weekly, dismantle the heavy reflectors and carry them down the tower and polish them "with dry rouge and chamois."[6] Scratches on any glass surface or prism attracted soot and required rubbing until the scratches disappeared.

❹ Fill the whale oil, coal oil, or paraffin (kerosene) reservoirs and clear the feed lines of debris. If the whale oil was of inferior quality, it had to be filtered. Short wicks had to be replaced.

❺ Oil and wind the rotating clockwork lamp apparatus and make it ready for the evening's start-up. As required, the clockwork springs had to be adjusted, as dampness or tarnish on any brass surface altered the accurate "flashing" sequence of the lamp. Records of any adjustment had to be noted in the logbook and had to conform to specified recommendations detailed in the Lightkeeper's Rules and Regulations.

❻ Note any broken and/or spare parts for the lamps, lenses, prisms, clockwork gear, and fuel-pumps logbook. Extra parts had to be ordered such that they were on hand.

❼ Clean and oil all the parts of the hand-pumped foghorn as necessary. If the foghorn was a compressed-air diaphone, all oil-reservoirs on the diesel or steam-engine compressors—the pistons, cylinders, and connecting rods—had to be oiled or kept filled. The fuel tank for the diesel engine required filling, and if the fuel was of poor quality, it, too, had to be filtered.

❽ Note any maintenance of the steam or diesel engines daily in a special logbook.

❾ Note any foghorn and/or diaphone maintenance daily in a special logbook. It was a serious offence if any piece of machinery failed to operate when required.

❶❶ Monitor passing traffic and note in the main logbook. That meant light keepers had to become proficient in flag semaphore, enabling them to communicate directly (if close enough) with passing ships. All messages had to be noted in the log. By 1906, a working knowledge of Morse code telegraphy was required. By the 1930s, a marine radio-operator's licence was also required.

❶❶ Submit monthly reports to the federal Department of Marine and Fisheries.

❶❷ Submit lists of required foodstuffs and other critical items to the lighthouse agent in Victoria in a timely enough manner so they can be included on the monthly supply ship. Storms often meant the supply ship didn't come on time, so self-sufficiency, especially in winter, was the key.

During the night, a light keeper had to:

❶ Remove the lamp curtains around the lamp room and light the lamps one hour before sunset. The rotating lamp housing was started and time had to be noted in the log.

❷ Trim lamp wick every three hours all through the night, "taking particular care that they were exactly even on the top."[7]

❸ Wind the clockwork rotating apparatus every three hours, all through the night.

❹ Respond to vessels in distress by reporting such messages to the coast guard. Give aid directly, if possible.

Throughout the year, the light keeper had to:

❶ Keep the lighthouse grounds immaculate, keeping the pathways clean, the grass trimmed, and lawns weed-free. All flower-beds required regular watering and weeding. All fences had to be white-washed regularly and kept in proper repair. It was expected that all tools and ancillary equipment would be properly maintained. The funds allocated for maintenance were strictly controlled.

❷ Keep a vegetable garden if soil conditions allowed. This was especially important if children were on the station. If the light keeper kept a cow, it was expected that her domicile would be cleaned daily.

❸ Cut wood for winter and always stack the woodpile neatly. Until the light keepers organized themselves into an association in the 1940s, costs of heating-fuel (wood, coal, etc.) and foodstuffs were borne from the keeper's salary.

❹ Paint the tower keeper's dwelling, machine sheds, and all out-buildings every two years and keep all trim bright and rot-free. The standard colours were red and white.

A LIGHT KEEPER'S SALARY THROUGH THE AGES

In 1854, an assistant light keeper was paid $25 per year.

In 1871, the Race Rocks Lighthouse keeper was paid $125 per year.

In 1884, a master light keeper was paid an average annual wage of $400.

In 1914, James Sadler, light keeper at Quatsino Lighthouse, was paid $540.

In 1916, after arguing that he was unable to support his family on that amount, Sadler's salary was raised to $876 per year.

In 1924, Quatsino light keeper Alfred Dickenson was paid $1,100 per year.[8]

In 1971, the average salary of a BC light keeper was $6,500 per year, "the lowest wages paid to any civil servants at the time."[9]

In 1988, the average annual salary for light keepers in Canada was $23,500.

▲ *James Bruton painting the light tower.* COURTESY OF S. BRUTON

TWENTY-FIVE

ISLAND LIGHTHOUSES
of SOUTHWESTERN BC

CAPE SCOTT—25

PULTENEY POINT—23

QUATSINO—24

VANCOUVER ISLAND

CAPE MUDGE—15

NOOTKA—22

ESTEVAN POINT—21

CHROME ISLAND—14   SISTERS ISLETS—13

BALLENAS ISLAND—12

LENNARD ISLAND—20

ENTRANCE ISLAND—11

AMPHITRITE POINT—19

PORLIER PASS—10

ACTIVE PASS—8

N

CAPE BEALE—18

PORTLOCK POINT—9   EAST POINT—7

PACHENA POINT—17

CARMANAH POINT—16

FIDDLE REEF—6   DISCOVERY ISLAND—5

PACIFIC OCEAN

TRIAL ISLANDS—4

SHERINGHAM POINT—1   FISGARD—3

RACE ROCKS—2

WASHINGTON

SHERINGHAM POINT

LAT 48°22′37″N, **LONG** 123°56′16″W

ACCESSIBILITY ❷ Still Easy

GETTING THERE Sheringham Point Lighthouse is located on the Strait of Juan de Fuca, in the village of Shirley, forty-five kilometres west of Victoria, just west of Sooke. Complete with attached buttresses, this beautiful, classic lighthouse is a marvel to behold. Visitors are welcome; a parking lot is adjacent.

Although the interior of the light tower is closed, the Sheringham Point Lighthouse Preservation Society plans to restore the whole site. Even as it is, the Sheringham Lighthouse is magnificent, and the view of it standing tall above the rocky shore will remind you that the impulse to serve once loomed large all along the Strait of Juan de Fuca and beyond to our vast Pacific coastal shores.

From Sooke, take Highway 14 (the West Coast Road) west for fifteen kilometres. Once past the Fire Hall in the village of Shirley, be on the lookout for Sheringham Point Road. Turn left (south) on Sheringham Point Road. On a rise immediately after the turn (on your right), you'll see the Shirley Delicious Cafe, owned by friendly locals Sheena Mercier and Phillip Da Preez. The cafe signals that you are minutes away from an architectural treasure. Grab a coffee on your way down to the lighthouse and perhaps stop and have lunch there on your way out. Shirley Delicious specializes in gluten-free and vegetarian options . . . and the food is wonderful.

Follow the Sheringham Point Road down to the gravel parking lot (a turnabout) at its end. From there, a short, grassy trail leads to the lighthouse, which soon becomes visible though the trees. Once there, the rocky promontory upon which the light stands will take your breath away. See if you can find the outline of the keeper's house and the bomb shelter behind it. On the weather side of the light, the snow-capped Hurricane Ridge of the Olympic Mountains across the Strait of Juan de Fuca begs for a photograph.

The best way to get to the Sheringham Point Lighthouse, however, is by bicycle along the Galloping Goose Trail from

▲ *Exact cartographic location marker, Sheringham Point.*

Victoria to Sooke. Stop for lunch at Royal Roads University en route. Cycle there during the week because the highway from Sooke to Shirley (though little used) has no paved shoulder, so take care. The best way is to make it an overnight cycling adventure, as Sooke abounds in inexpensive B&Bs. That way you'll have time to explore Whiffen Spit, the boardwalk, and the Sooke Region Museum. The Sooke Potholes are just a short cycling jaunt away, before you return to Victoria the next day.

THE WEIRD Eustace Arden, the keeper at Sheringham Point Lighthouse during World War II, was required to draw the black-out curtains on all the windows of the station with interior illumination, every night, from 1941 to 1945.

THE NAME For centuries before first contact, the Ditidaht First Nation called the area around Sheringham Point *p'aachiida*, or "seafoam-on-rocks."[10] In 1790, the Spanish gave it their own name, Punta de San Eusebio, until the British firmly established sovereignty in the nineteenth century. In 1846, Captain Kellett of the Royal Navy survey ship HMS *Herald* renamed it again as Sheringham Point after William Sheringham, his vice admiral back in England. Sheringham never even saw the place.[11]

After British Columbia joined Confederation in 1871, settlement began in earnest. By the 1880s, land around Sheringham Point was being pre-empted for farming, finally acquiring the status of a village. But the name Sheringham Point was too long to fit on a postage stamp when, in 1893, the place acquired its own post office. Mrs. Clark, wife of the new postmaster, Edwin Clark, suggested the name Shirley, after her own native village and chapelry near Southampton, Hampshire, England.[12] Edwin Clark believed a boom was coming and bought up 174 acres of surrounding land in 1910 for $174, which amounted to $1 per acre.[13]

DESIGN AND CONSTRUCTION   By 1900, William P. Anderson had become the Arthur Erickson of lighthouse architecture in Canada. Anderson was born in Lévis, Quebec, in 1851 and joined the Canadian Militia at fourteen. He fought against the Fenians, whose goal during the 1860s was to pressure Britain to withdraw from Ireland by raiding local customs houses and garrisons in "Upper Canada." At twenty-two, Anderson became a commander with the Ottawa Rifles. A year later he became a railway surveyor, then joined the Department of Marine and Fisheries. He rose quickly through the ranks to become its chief lighthouse designer. Colonel Anderson's military career deeply influenced his ideas about the construction of secure, coastal structures. In all, he designed some 355 technically advanced, robust, and truly beautiful light stations situated on Canada's two coasts and around the Great Lakes.

Colonel Anderson became best known for his striking flying-buttress light towers at Belle Isle (Newfoundland and Labrador), Île-d'Anticosti (Quebec), Lake Superior, and Estevan Point (Vancouver Island). The Sheringham Point Lighthouse takes stylistic inspiration from these sturdy structures.

When the SS *Valencia* steamed onto a reef some 45 metres from shore between Pachena Bay and Carmanah Point in January 1906, losing 126 lives to the surf, a Commission of Enquiry determined that more lighthouses were required on the west coast of Vancouver Island. The light station at Sheringham Point was built in response to this tragedy. The term "graveyard of the Pacific" suddenly gained an awful legitimacy.

In 1911, Edwin Clark sold four acres of his land at Sheringham Point to the federal government for $50 per acre. Within a year Clark had paid off his acreage and made a tidy profit, and Canada gained the ground for a new important light station.[14]

Begun in the spring of 1912, the Sheringham Lighthouse was a hexagonal reinforced-concrete structure 19.5 metres high

▲ *Spiral staircase, Sheringham.* John Walls

with six, graceful pilaster-like buttresses. Cost of the tower: the fog-alarm building with its diesel, compressed-air generator; the boathouse; and the keeper's dwelling at the time came to $9,000. Another $12,000 was spent for the purchase, shipping and installation of a large, third-order Fresnel-lens lamp, which shone out into the Strait of Juan de Fuca for some twenty-four kilometres.[15]

In order for the five-ton lamp apparatus to rotate more easily in the lamp room, it was "floated" on liquid mercury to minimize friction. The rotating mechanism with its clockwork weights and pulleys needed winding every three hours from dusk to dawn, each day.

THE KEEPERS Eustace Arden lit the lamp for the first time on September 30, 1912, and, in spite of all the winding, he loved the place. There were six noisy keeper's children and cows roaming free all over the place, and the uptight, business-minded next-door neighbour, Edwin Clark, tried hard to have them removed from the station. He failed, and the Arden family happily remained at Sheringham Point for over thirty-three years.[16]

Two world wars left an indelible imprint on the Canadian lighthouse psyche. The alleged enemy attack on Estevan Lighthouse in June 1942 alerted the Department of Marine to get ready to defend the isolated, outer-coast stations. In the early 1960s, when the Cold War threatened to overheat, Ottawa built several bomb shelters at several lighthouses near Victoria (including Sheringham and Discovery). Ostensibly constructed to protect light keepers from nuclear fallout, the shelter at Sheringham Point was a very strange affair indeed.

It was little more than a flat-roofed, concrete-block root cellar, half dug into the ground. With 0.5-metre-thick walls, it was smaller inside than a bedroom. It allowed for only two bunk beds and little else—and that was the problem. The Department of Marine and Fisheries demanded that the shelters be used solely by the light keeper and his assistant, excluding family members. According on the daughter of a former Sheringham keeper, "The door was to be bolted shut from the inside for that reason."[17] That was but one of Ottawa's nonsensical, if not depraved, rules. By the time James Bruton arrived at Sheringham Point in 1968, Cold War paranoia was fading and the edict had been long ignored. James turned his minuscule shelter into a mushroom farm, which failed, and the silly structure was torn down and filled in.

James Bruton served nearly twenty years at Sheringham Point, retiring in 1986 when electrification and de-staffing began in earnest. With his wife and four children, Bruton witnessed the golden age of light keeping on this coast. In one year he welcomed over four thousand curious and respectful visitors.[18] Automation and the de-staffing of the stations in the 1990s killed public awareness of the importance the light stations, so one of James's daughters,

▲ *Wedding party on lamp gallery, December 4, 1976.* COURTESY OF S. BRUTON

Elanie, set out to teach later generations about life on the manned station by becoming a founding member of the Sheringham Point Lighthouse Preservation Society.

Elanie's sister Sharon Kerrigan-Bruton was married at Sheringham Point Lighthouse on December 4, 1976. That day, they managed to cram sixteen family members, friends, and the preacher all together in the lamp room at the top of the tower— which was against the rules. Hardly bigger than a closet, the place rocked with laughter. James Bruton further broke regula-tions by painting the inside of the tower a matrimonial royal blue (instead of regulation grey), just for the wedding. He also had his citizens' band radio hooked up to speakers at ground level and broadcast the whole ceremony to more guests standing

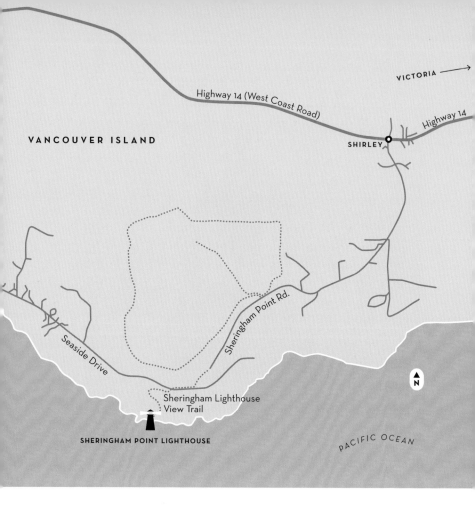

and waiting below. Three photographers stopped in at a nearby pub in Sooke to ask directions and never made it to the wedding. What a party![19]

Along with their other duties, a light keeper and his assistant were required, every two years, to paint the exterior roofs of their dwellings, the tower, and other outbuildings on their stations. The colour demanded for the roofs was a brilliant red. The trouble was that in those early years, the paint was lead based. As the dangers of lead poisoning became known, Ottawa duly passed on that knowledge to the keepers. By then, however, many light keepers had been figuratively immersing themselves in the poisonous stuff for decades. When James Bruton got sick, Sharon Kerrigan-Bruton said of her keeper-father, "It was no wonder when he got leukemia."[20]

Another heavy metal found in abundance on all light stations from 1900 to 1980 was liquid mercury in the form of hundreds of tiny balls that were used to float the Fresnel-lamp apparatus so that it could be rotated more easily by a simple clockwork drive. During those years, an untold number of keepers may have developed Minamata disease—a neurological syndrome caused by mercury poisoning that can lead to mental impairment, paralysis, coma, and death. Records of those keepers who caught Minamata disease through their handling of mercury were simply not kept, and Ottawa did not encourage light keepers who were ill to take time off to seek medical attention. Without records or a physician tracking an illness, the government escaped responsibility and ultimately the payment of any compensation for keepers' untimely deaths.[21]

▲ *Wildlife from sea and shore surrounds the stations.*

RACE ROCKS

LAT 49° 18′ 01″ N, **LONG** 123° 32′ 02″ W

ACCESSIBILITY ⑤ Really, Really Hard

GETTING THERE Unless you have the required permit or have arranged a ride with those running the Race Rocks Ecological Reserve, or are passing close by on a whale-watching venture or other tour, don't go. Especially, don't go in a kayak without nearby water-borne support. Even though it's only a short distance from Bentinck Island (which is off limits), or Rocky Point on Vancouver Island, the currents around Race Rocks are deadly. If, however, you can have the opportunity to join a decidedly safe tour to Race Rocks, take it.

THE WEIRD The story that the Race Rocks Lighthouse was built from stone quarried in Scotland and sent to the Pacific Coast as ballast in sailing ships, may be just that—more yarn than truth. Doubts began to surface soon after construction was complete.

Historian Dale Mumford wrote that not only would it have been extremely dangerous to ship huge precut stone blocks as sailing-ship ballast, but it would have also been completely unworkable. He noted that most ballast was shingle or pig iron, and had to be readily removable from the hold should a ship require careening or dry-docking. Ever efficient and safety-minded, the Royal Navy, which helped select the site, would have certainly questioned the cut-stone-as-ballast plan. In 1860, J. Pemberton, a surveyor for the Colony of Vancouver Island, wrote, "Brick would be preferable and [blue-stone] granite, quarried on the spot, is excellent." No early books, not even Captain John Walbran's *British Columbia Coast Names*, have confirmed the original story. Only Thomas Appleton's *History of the Canadian Coast Guard* states, "Race Rocks is constructed in stone quarried in Scotland and sent by sailing ship around Cape Horn." Others have written that the stone was quarried on Gabriola Island. Go figure.[22]

One thing is certain. The lime-coloured tower proved difficult to see in certain light conditions, so George Davies, the first light keeper at Race Rocks, made the highly textured, rough-hewn stone tower strikingly visible by painting alternating black-and-white wide bands around it from its base to its top. The distinctive stripes remain.

THE NAME Race Rocks is a cluster of low, bare rocks approximately 1.6 kilometres from Bentinck Island and the southeastern tip of Vancouver Island. The whole group of rocky islets is less than one square kilometre. The outermost and largest islet is called Great Race. It's barely three acres in size and is only seven metres above mean sea level. It is upon Great Race that the Race Rocks Lighthouse is constructed. Other nearby rocky outcroppings are smaller and lower, and several are completely awash at high tide. The tidal flow around Race Rocks is fierce and, as Royal Navy commander Captain Kellett wrote in 1846, "it is a perfect race."

▲ *Steller sea lions challenge each other for turf.*

From the Pacific Ocean, the Strait of Juan de Fuca narrows considerably from its mouth to the southern tip of Vancouver Island. The tidal flow sweeps through this constriction with great speed. Moreover, just off Race Rocks, the sea bottom shallows quickly. The result is that the tidal currents between Bentinck Island and Vancouver Island reach up to nine knots under normal conditions. During storms, even faster, more dangerous tidal races occur, complete with fearsome standing waves.

In 1870, the sailing directions for the North Pacific Ocean warned mariners that even in light winds, a sailing vessel, when eastwards of the islands, should give Race Rocks an especially wide berth because the tide will move inexorably towards the Rocks, carrying ships with it and with little headway.[23]

DESIGN AND CONSTRUCTION Captains Richards and Fulford of the Royal Navy, along with Vancouver Island's harbour master J. Nagle and Surveyor General Joseph Pemberton, chose the sites for the Race Rocks and Fisgard Lighthouses together. This collaboration was critical in that the approaches to the Esquimalt Navy Base and Victoria Harbour had to be absolutely clear. The locations of both lighthouses undoubtedly favoured the Royal Navy because all vessels rounding Race Rocks Lighthouse saw the naval base immediately, and a direct bearing upon the Fisgard Lighthouse at Esquimalt Harbour's entrance kept all ships of Her Majesty's service clear of danger.

The British government appropriated £7,000 for the two lighthouses, and work began in 1859. Site manager Joseph Pemberton was a tough taskmaster, because on April 7, 1860, contractor John Morris reported that twelve stonecutters were already on Great Race along with a cook and all stores necessary to finish the job by the end of that year. They accomplished their task because in late December 1860, Race Rocks Lighthouse became operational. With crew from HMS *Topaz* assisting in the construction, the gang at Race Rocks worked like beavers to beat their rival workers constructing the Fisgard Lighthouse. Sadly for them, Fisgard beat them at their task by just over a month.[24]

The stone tower was twenty-four metres above mean sea level. The focal plane was thirty-five metres. Chance Brothers of Birmingham made the bright second-order Fresnel lamp assembly, and was lit for the first time on December 26, 1860, becoming the second operational lighthouse on the BC coast.

THE KEEPERS Keeper George Davies, his wife, Rosina, and their three children arrived from Britain in late 1860, but his new posting would underscore the tragedies that often befell many of the early light keepers on this coast. On Christmas Day 1865, George and Rosina eagerly awaited the arrival of long-missed family from England, when George's brother-in-law, Warner, his wife, and three other old friends hove into view in a small boat. Suddenly, six metres away from the shore, the boat became

▲ *Keeper George Davies's hand-painted tower can be seen from Olympic Peninsula in the US.*

caught in a riptide and capsized. One of their friends was seen struggling, shouting hysterically as he drifted away in the cold current. Without rope or life rings handy, everyone in the boat perished. Days before, Joseph Pemberton had taken the station boat to Victoria and did not return in time to prevent the tragedy.

A year later, George Davies became desperately ill. Rosina flew a distress signal from the flagstaff for two weeks to no avail. George died, without medical intervention, on December 14, 1866.

In 1867, the Colony paid Davies's replacement, T. Argyle, an annual salary of $630. The Admiralty added another $900 to his salary for supplies. In 1871, when British Columbia joined Confederation, the Royal Navy duly cancelled the supply money.

Ottawa never took up the slack and even dropped Argyle's wages to $125 annually. But Argyle got the last laugh. He found an unknown wreck full of unclaimed treasures nearby and spent a goodly part of his later life lavishly spending his gold sovereigns. He died happy and flush in 1888.[25]

Though important, the lighthouse at Race Rocks helped only marginally. It was the fog that compounded the effect of the terrible tidal flow. Many ships were lost near Race Rocks, with many human casualties, though none more tragic than the sinking of the *Sechelt* ferry in 1911:

- *Nichola Biddle*—sank, January 5, 1867
- *Swordfish*—sank, November 6, 1877

- *Rosedale*—sank, December 12, 1882
- *Barnard Castle*—ran aground, November 2, 1886
- *Sechelt* (ferry)—sank, March 24, 1911 (fifty lives lost)
- *Siberian Prince*—ran aground, July 5, 1923
- *Eemdijk*—ran aground, November 2, 1925
- *Empress of Canada*—ran aground, October 13, 1925

A 1927 investigation proved that a turn-of-the-century fog-horn shed was placed too near the Race Rocks light tower, and this, along with the surrounding topography, created a "dead zone" that prevented the horn from being heard on certain bearings by ships at sea. Later that year, Race Rocks was fitted with British Columbia's first radio beacon.

In 1939, the Royal Canadian Navy established a Port War Signal Station at Race Rocks, adjacent to the lighthouse. Three radio-telegraphers and three signalmen were sent to Great Race Rock to report all ship movements directly to naval headquarters in Esquimalt. Light keeper Andrew Ritchie and his wife, Kathleen, were flabbergasted that the men were sent out to live in tents. Winter gales drove them into the leaky boathouse on the station. Yet even here, the men had to use the wood from their provision boxes to nail to the walls of the boathouse for further protection from the hurricane-driven horizontal spray. Conditions were so fierce that in March 1940, the men were moved to the newly built Churchill Port War Signal Station on Mary Hill at Rocky Point, Metchosin. Discovery Island Lighthouse, east of Oak Bay, also accommodated a Port War Signal Station on its grounds for the duration of the war.[26]

In 1980, after an initiative by students at Victoria's Pearson College, part of the Race Rocks Islets (and surrounding waters) were formally designated as Race Rocks Ecological Reserve. In 1997, the Canadian Coast Guard de-staffed the lighthouse.

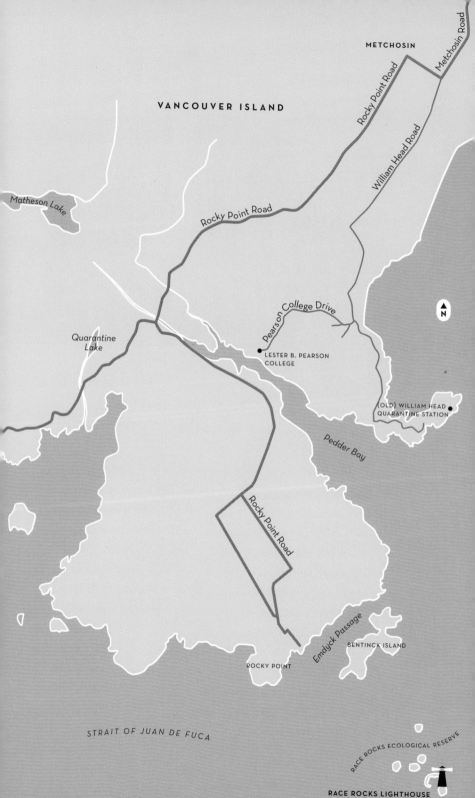

3

FISGARD

LAT 48°25′38″ N, **LONG** 123°27′17″ W

ACCESSIBILITY **1** Dead Easy

GETTING THERE If you are in Victoria, visiting Fisgard Lighthouse is a must. It's a short, easy drive (fourteen kilometres) from downtown Victoria along Highway 1. At Colwood, turn onto Highway 1A, then left on Ocean Boulevard. There is also transit service directly from downtown Victoria to nearby Ocean Boulevard, and signs point the direction of the short walk to the light. Both Fisgard Lighthouse and the gun battery at Fort Rodd Hill are national historic sites and fully integrated with an interpretive centre, exhibits, and tours.

Better yet, bicycle along the Galloping Goose Trail, a dedicated bicycle-only pathway from Victoria. En route, at Royal Roads University, visit Hatley Castle and have lunch in the (licensed) cafeteria. Then find Ocean Boulevard and follow the signs. It's a day trip you will remember, and it will inspire you to do more lighthouse-spotting on Vancouver Island and the nearby Gulf Islands.

THE WEIRD Talk about embarrassing! At the entrance to Esquimalt Harbour, Britain's Royal Navy base on Canada's west coast from 1842–65, there is a rock. And it's very close to Fisgard Lighthouse. It was found the hard way by HMS *Bacchante,* the flagship of Rear Admiral Sir Thomas Maitland, a distinguished and starchy aristocrat who served as the commander-in-chief of the Esquimalt station from 1860 to 1862. During his naval career, Maitland won naval honours in the 1840 seizures of Canton, Chusan, Amoy, and Shanghai and was rewarded for increasing the range of influence of the British Empire. His flagship, a steam-powered screw sailing ship, struck the rock upon entering Esquimalt Harbour on July 22, 1862. Fortunately for HMS *Bacchante's* captain, Maitland was not on board that particular day; otherwise, its hapless skipper might have found himself rowing a wherry across the River Thames.[27]

THE NAME Fisgard Lighthouse is named after HMS *Fisgard,* a forty-two-gun Royal Navy frigate that was stationed at the Esquimalt base from 1844 to 1847. "Esquimalt" is an English language derivative of the Coast Salish word *es-whoy-malth,* meaning "a place where the water shoals." The Songhees people lived in the area long before first contact and spoke a North Straits Salish dialect called Lekwungen. In July 1789, the small British trading sloop *Princess Royal* was seized by the Spaniards, who had just taken possession of Nootka. The ship, its crew, and its cargo were captured soon after entering Nootka Sound. Sub-Lieutenant Manuel Quimper became Nootka's new master and was instructed by the Spanish

▲ *"Excuse me?"*

viceroy to chart the whole coast, south of the place. Quimper sailed into Esquimalt and named it Puerto de Córdova, but the Nootka convention ceded it to Britain in 1794, changing Quimper's appellation to Esquimalt Harbour in the mid-nineteenth century.

DESIGN AND CONSTRUCTION   The real architect of Fisgard Lighthouse, the Fort Rodd Hill gun battery, and the Esquimalt naval station was the very real threat of war with America and Russia. Britain had moved its Pacific naval squadron from Valparaíso, Chile, to Esquimalt in part to avoid being drawn into a war between Chile, Peru, and Spain over the Chincha Islands (1864). In truth, the Royal Navy had been in Esquimalt since the 1840s, and Governor Douglas supported the construction of Fisgard and Race Rocks Lighthouses in the midst of the confusion over the 1846 Oregon boundary dispute, the 1858 Fraser River Gold Rush, and the San Juan Islands "Pig War" in 1859.

In consequence, Fisgard Lighthouse became symbolic of the British naval and military presence on the Northwest Coast and

▲ *The big guns guard the causeway, lighthouse, and Esquimalt Harbour.*

stood vigilant towards Russia's territorial activities in the Crimea (1854), the Balkans (1855–70), and in the Alaska boundary dispute (1903). If there was to be a lighthouse guarding Esquimalt, it had to be a good one.

Fisgard Lighthouse is an architectural anomaly on the west coast. It is a conical white brick tower resting upon a granite base some sixteen metres above mean sea level. When it was built, the pièce de résistance was its Chance Brothers of Birmingham–made, fourth-order light apparatus, high in the lamp gallery, which rotated and rested upon a friction-less bath of mercury. Its focal plane range directed its beam of light some sixteen kilometres, into the Strait of Juan de Fuca.[28] In February 1929, Fisgard's old light was replaced, and in the 1940s, the acetylene-powered lamp was replaced again by an electric one.

Aside from its Gothic revival architectural features, includ-ing the pointed-arch windows of both the lighthouse and the keeper's dwelling and in the brick corbelling of the tower itself, one of the most interesting features of Fisgard Lighthouse is its internal staircase—a beautiful, ornate wrought-iron spiral staircase that was designed and produced in San Francisco (the design alone cost over $300).

THE KEEPERS Before he was the keeper of Race Rocks Lighthouse, George Davies—newly arrived from Britain with his wife, Rosina, and their three children—was stationed at Fisgard. The voyage out to Victoria on the sailing ship *Grecian* took over seven months, with Fisgard's lamp apparatus firmly stowed in the ship's hold. Upon arrival, Davies discovered that many of the apparatus's glass fittings had been smashed by the pounding of the seas and perhaps by a careless loading crew. Moreover, parts of the lamp's iron structure had rusted.[29] Despite the setback, Davies lit the Fisgard light on November 16, 1860, and its illustrious career as the first lighthouse on Canada's west coast began. He moved to Race Rocks in 1861.

Nearly twenty years later, on August 5, 1879, Fisgard's third keeper, William Bevis, died while on duty. For four months afterwards, Bevis's wife and nineteen-year-old niece kept the lamp burning, from 4:00 p.m. daily to 8:00 a.m. the next morning. When Ottawa found out, the lighthouse agent in Victoria sent out a terse reply: "It is against the rules of the Dept. to place women in charge of lighthouses."[30] Henry Cogan replaced the two women on January 6, 1880.

In 1898, Joseph Dare (Fisgard's keeper in 1884) drowned while rowing his skiff out to the lighthouse in a storm. (In 1950, a causeway was constructed from the Fort Rodd Hill gun battery across to the lighthouse. It was said that the causeway was built over the World War II torpedo-net stretched across from the shore at Fort Rodd Hill out to the station to protect the base from enemy attack should the signalmen at the Port War Signal

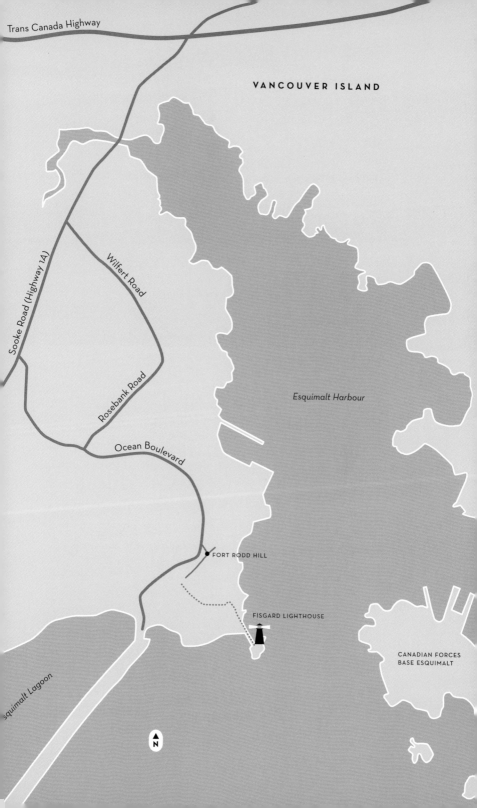

▲ *We stand on guard for thee.*

Stations at Race Rocks or Discovery Island Lighthouses fall asleep at the switch.)

Life at Fisgard was far from a sweet posting, and the Victorian sense of duty wasn't always followed to the letter. William Cormack, Joseph Dare's replacement, held the record for the shortest time that a light keeper remained at a station in Canada. Cormack resigned after only twelve days on the job. In his letter of resignation he cited his reasons as "boredom and monotony."[31] Go figure.

TRIAL ISLANDS

LAT 48°23′41″ N, **LONG** 123°18′22″ W

ACCESSIBILITY ❹ Hard

GETTING THERE   Getting to the Trial Islands by kayak is not for duffers. You must be of demonstrable competence, know how to read the tide-and-current tables, and be certain of the weather. The closest proper boat-launching ramp is at Cattle Point in Oak Bay. If you are an inexperienced kayaker, consider taking a whale-watching tour from Victoria instead. These tours often pass close to the Trial Islands Lighthouse.

If you are dead keen and determined to explore directly, the Trial Islands are now designated as an ecological reserve, and permission to land is required. Under the aegis of Parks Canada, the islands are home to over twenty significantly rare plant species. Harbour seals use the rocky outcroppings as resting and birthing grounds. Bald eagles abound.

▲ *"I'm watching everything you're doing—so stop it!"*

THE WEIRD Years before a lighthouse was built on the Trial Islands, the place already had a troubling reputation. John Livermore (a.k.a. "Whiskey John" or "Liverpool Jack") was an American hotel keeper turned bootlegger, who, in the ten years he spent in Victoria, "must have served out fifty short terms of imprisonment for selling whiskey to Siwashes."[32]

Known, too, for his flair in dodging the assizes, Livermore soon figured out a scheme using the Trial Islands. He believed the islands' treacherous currents would thwart those chasing him, so he pirated some 180 gallons of his best black-market booze and began a roaring trade with passing Natives. All went well until September 1864 when, with truncheons in hand, the Victoria Constabulary caught the swaggering yokel red-handed. Livermore was given yet another sentence. When he died five years later, his obituary read, "Whiskey John excelled as a salesman among the Indians and has probably poisoned more Natives than any other man, living or dead."[33]

▲ *Light station from the Strait of Juan de Fuca. Note the solar panel and fog horn shed near the water.*

THE NAME The Trial Islands stand at the very southeastern tip of Vancouver Island and mark roughly the turning point where the Strait of Juan de Fuca becomes Georgia Strait. The tidal flow, often against the prevailing westerlies, makes that turning a hair-raising experience, even for experienced mariners. Such difficulties continued to dog the reputation of the Trial Islands as they took on imperial responsibility.

After the Royal Navy closed its Pacific Station in Valparaíso, Chile, Admiralty sailing-ships were regularly sent for a refit to the navy's new dockyard in Esquimalt. Before returning to their various stations around Britain's Pacific empire, all ships were first required to make a "sea trial." In the 1860s, short-tacking full-rigged frigates, such as HMS *Ganges*, to the Trial Islands and back, against stiff headwinds, strong currents, and steep seas, tested the mettle of all iron men and wooden ships before they answered the call of Her Majesty's Imperial Service. Such formidable sea trials were the making of the Royal Navy. They made a statement about the navy's confidence in its new Esquimalt facility and its respect for the treacherous waters of this coast. The name "Enterprise Channel" is apt. This narrow, boisterous passage between Trial Islands and Vancouver Island is named after the HBC paddle-wheeler *Enterprise*. It was lost in a collision with the steamer *R.P. Rithet* in the vicinity of the islands in 1888.[34]

DESIGN AND CONSTRUCTION   The turn of the twentieth century saw a veritable explosion in the design and construction of lighthouses on Canada's west coast, and a few contractors became both dependable and adept at their task. Although it would also serve the interests of a new province's booming economy, the location and presence of the light at Staines Point, the highest point on the largest of the small islands, no doubt reflected the Royal Navy's imperial legacy. So any lighthouse placed there had to be substantial. George Frost of Nanaimo and Victoria had already established a fine reputation in building Carmanah Point and Lucy Island light stations, so the generous $12,000 contract went to him.

▲ *A black oystercatcher spotting lunch.*

In 1905, concrete foundations were poured for the light tower and the attached keeper's residence. A square (nine-by-nine-metre) wooden two-storey shingled residence soon emerged with a square lamp gallery protruding from its roof. A fixed white oil-lantern would have to suffice as the beacon, until a brighter, fourth-order Chance Brothers lamp with a Fresnel lens arrived from Birmingham, England, in September 1906. By the 1920s, the Trial Islands Lighthouse even had a telephone.

The Trial Islands are little more than craggy, treeless outcroppings where Juan de Fuca and Georgia Straits merge. Fresh water was not readily available, so Frost constructed a twenty-two-cubic-metre cistern beneath the keeper's kitchen. He also planned to build a separate foghorn building nearer the water's edge, housing a new, high-pitched, compressed-air set of diaphones. Until that installation was complete, the light keeper was given a hand-operated foghorn to use in response to a ship's whistle. The light keeper's response would establish a safe bearing for a ship somewhere off in the gloom, to miss the islands. Everything was ready by October 1906, but . . .

THE KEEPERS Harold Shorrock O'Kell, Trial Islands' first keeper (1906–31), received the order to hand-crank his foghorn too late, "since the *Twickenham*, a large and new steamer with a cargo of five thousand tons of sugar, had stranded itself in the vicinity a few days before the diaphones were installed."[35] O'Kell was completely blameless; he acted as soon as the order was issued. The Trial Islands Lighthouse had been called into action moments before it was ready.

O'Kell possessed the best qualities in a light keeper that Canada's lighthouse service could ever hope to find. He was an experienced mariner who knew the godforsaken temperament of the seas. As a young man, he lost a leg to its vagaries when a cable to a vessel he was towing snapped, recoiled, and "shattered his shin bone."[36] During the twenty-five years O'Kell spent at the Trial Islands Lighthouse, he hobbled about on his peg leg and transported tons of topsoil to the island in his rowboat. He created a garden, built planters, and even towed over a cow from Oak Bay on a makeshift platform so his wife and new baby would have a continuing supply of fresh milk. Ever aware of the imminent shortage of fresh water, "The O'Kells often rowed to town for a bath to conserve water for their parched and precious flowers."[37] In his light-keeping duties, O'Kell showed the same kind of creativity and reliability that made his island workplace a showpiece. Ottawa's lighthouse agent in Victoria, James Gaudin, praised his qualities and his long service.

During World War II, the Department of National Defence set about removing the telephone link to the Trial Islands Lighthouse, claiming the cable was needed elsewhere to better serve the search-and-rescue services of Canada's coastal war effort. Many of the federal lighthouse agents stationed across the country were obedient bureaucrats and only too happy to do Ottawa's bidding. But Victoria's lighthouse agent at the time, Tom Morrison, was of a different ilk and began a campaign to save the Trial Islands phone cable. Writing to his national mandarins, Morrison argued that the light station was already deeply involved in search-and-rescue missions and had been for some time.

In 1944, light keeper Samuel Dondale saved five crew from a sailing yacht that had been smashed to pieces on the island during a vicious storm. Somehow the keeper made his way to the wreck, administered first aid, and through the fury helped move them to his little house above the raging sea. There, Dondale discovered that one of the crew was critically injured and, as the navy couldn't make a landing during the storm, "he was given medical advice over the phone to treat him."[38] The man survived, and the

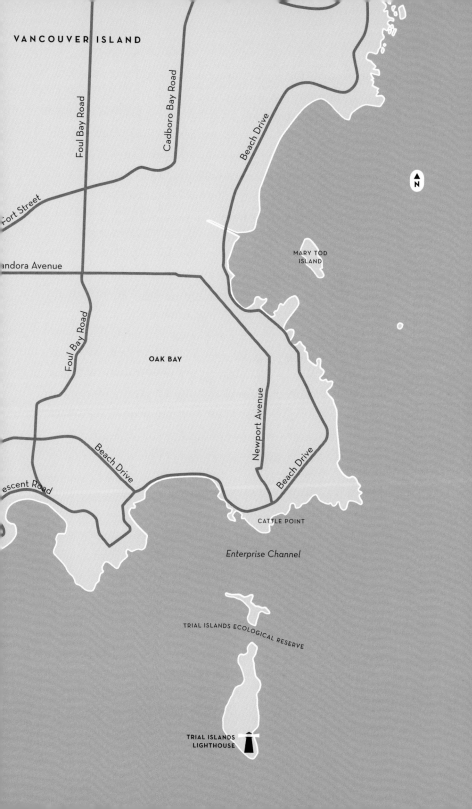

telephone cable remained to serve those in peril about the Trial Islands for another day.

In 1997, light keeper Iain Colquhoun saved the lives of James Weitman and Jeff Beitz who found themselves in trouble in the riptides less than a kilometre south of the lighthouse. Just finishing a cup of tea, assistant keeper Kathy Doyle saw an empty kayak out in the strait. Binoculars confirmed that there were indeed two kayaks, and one of the paddlers was in the water. Colquhoun set out for them through heavy seas in the station boat as Doyle phoned the coast guard. Then she proceeded to guide her boss to the scene using the shortwave radio. James Weitman was severely hypothermic when Iain pulled him from the water; his best friend, Jeff Beitz, was terror-struck, cold, and helpless.[39]

In September 2009, the Canadian government announced that the Trial Islands Lighthouse would be de-staffed, "as part of a cost-saving plan to eliminate all light keeper positions."[40] Just two months before, on June 7, 2009, five kayakers were rescued from the waters off the Trial Islands by the coast guard: "After a group of 12 kayakers were swamped by [the wake] of a passing powerboat. One kayaker was able to swim to shore, but she and four others were taken to hospital and treated for hypothermia."[41] Light keeper Meredith Dickman had spotted the victims in the water and notified authorities. What would have happened had the kayakers been swamped after the government's plan was in effect?

In 2012, after visiting manned stations in British Columbia, an American congressional committee recommended that de-staffing be stopped. The Standing Senate Committee on Fisheries and Oceans passed a resolution to have the government review its policy. The reprieve is still in effect at Trial Islands Lighthouse (and a few others) in 2015. But for how long?

DISCOVERY ISLAND

LAT 48°25′27″ N, **LONG** 123°13′32″ W

ACCESSIBILITY ❸ Moderate

GETTING THERE Discovery Island Marine Provincial Park is located a mere two nautical miles off Oak Bay and makes a wonderful trip for experienced kayakers. Begin your trip as slack tide (the period in which the tide is turning) begins. There are boat-launching ramps on Beach Avenue, at Cattle Point, and at the end of Ten Mile Point in Cadboro Bay. Getting there involves crossing Plumper Passage, past Fiddle Reef and the Chain Islets to Rudlin Bay, Sea Bird Point, and the lighthouse. En route you will see seals, sea lions, sea otters, and bald eagles. In summer, the waters are usually calm though riptides are common near Sea Bird Point, so be careful. If you are going over in a larger boat, be aware of several large unmarked rocks between Discovery Island and Oak Bay, the most dangerous being Virtue Rock, which has only sixty centimetres of water over it at chart datum. Carolina Rock, which dries at a metre above chart datum, lies just north of the Chain Islets.[42]

If you are sailing over, Rudlin Bay is the primary access to the park, but it's full of shoals and is exposed to southeast winds, which are rare in summer. Should a wind come up, there's a temporary anchorage at the western end of the bay.

Being a marine park, Discovery Island has numerous trails. Good campsites can be found at Pandora Hill near the lighthouse, not to mention wonderful views of Washington's Olympic Mountains. Two large food caches have been placed at the site for the lone wolf who lives on the island. For that reason, pets are not allowed.

THE WEIRD Let them eat cake! Two weeks before Christmas 1897, the Victoria *Daily Colonist* made the following phlegmatic announcement: "The Dominion steamer *Quadra* made an unsuccessful attempt yesterday to deliver winter provisions to the Discovery Island Lighthouse. The southeast gale rendered it impossible to effect a landing and the light keeper will just have to wait."[43]

Government location marker (left) *and warning* (right).

That Christmas, the lights of Oak Bay would have been clearly visible to the Discovery Island light keeper had he been standing on the island's southwestern corner. Yet, the well-heeled citizens of this burgeoning suburb of Victoria wouldn't have seen the light from their homes, their horse-drawn hacks, or the streetcars trundling along Oak Bay Avenue. But they would have known it was there. That Saturday evening, Oak Bay was just beginning to revel in its Christmas flourish, and most were likely settling in for another evening martini. How very English that the stalwart, rain-soaked light keeper would just have to wait.

"Harriet, my deah, how or-ful. By the way, have you seen the evening's paper?"

THE NAME Discovery Island belonged to the Songhees people long before the British showed up, and for generations it was known by the Lekwungen name *Thlchess*. It was named Discovery Island in 1846 by Captain Kellett of the survey ship HMS *Herald* in honour of George Vancouver's ship *Discovery*. The neighbouring island was named Chatham, after Vancouver's escort vessel, which voyaged with him on his 1792 exploration of the inner coast.[44] Ironically, Vancouver never went anywhere near Discovery Island and sailed instead up the eastern edge of Georgia Strait, more intent on finding a northern passage through to the Pacific.[45]

Being located at the confluence of the Strait of Juan de Fuca, Haro Strait, and Georgia Strait, Discovery Island rose to prominence with the Fraser River Gold Rush of 1858. During that whole summer, the American paddlewheel steamers *Seabird* and *Surprise* transported thousands of hopeful miners up "Fraser's River." When *Seabird* caught fire and was grounded on Discovery Island on September 7, 1858, there was an outcry for a lighthouse at Sea Bird Point. That clamour lasted nearly thirty years.

DESIGN AND CONSTRUCTION In 1885, Alex Rennie and Co. of Port Moody won the $2,300 federal contract to build a lighthouse on the southern tip of the Discovery Island. Unlike the more isolated light stations on the outer coast, the Discovery Island Lighthouse posting was considered a plum job, being little more than a nautical mile off British Columbia's newest cosmopolitan and cultured community.

The first tower was a pyramidal white wooden structure with a square base. It stood some twelve metres above the rocks at Sea Bird Point. The red lamp gallery crowned it and contained a sixth-order Fresnel-lens lamp, which shone out some twelve nautical miles into the inky blackness of the increasingly busy seaways.

THE KEEPERS In 1890, a smaller building was constructed nearer the shore's edge for a steam-powered foghorn. Yet during the foggy night of October 30, 1892, the horn failed to sound, and the steamer *Premier* missed certain disaster by centimetres thanks to the quick reflexes and local knowledge of its skipper, Captain Rudlin. On board that night was James Gaudin, the federal light-house agent who was stationed in Victoria. He knew that Richard Brinn, the station's first keeper, had hired an assistant whose task was to keep all the machinery and its attendant apparatus in good repair. As head man, Brinn was responsible and should have suffered the consequences. Gaudin fumed and complained to Ottawa over his incompetence. The lighthouse service, acting upon the directions of their federal mandarins, decided, however, that Brinn should keep his job.

It was known that Richard Brinn was not well from the outset. He was fifty-three years old and already feeble when posted to the Discovery Island Lighthouse. Some said he was not fired out of compassion for his age and condition. Others declared with more certainty that it was Ottawa's "unadulterated patronage" that gave him impunity and caused him to be left alone. Whatever

▲ *Discovery Light Station from Rudlin Bay.*

it was, Richard soon became seriously ill; he was hospitalized in 1901 and died later that year. All the while, his daughter Mary Ann Croft looked after her own two small children and ran the station, keeping its horns wailing and the light burning bright.

After Richard Brinn's death, several prominent Victorians petitioned Ottawa to make Mrs. Croft the official keeper. Although it was unheard of for a woman to be hired to this position at the time, her attention to the demands of the station during her father's long absence won the day. On April 9, 1902, Mary Ann Croft became Canada's first official female lighthouse keeper. Her assistant, Henry Cumner Watts, left the service.

In 1906, a brighter fourth-order Chance Brothers lamp replaced the old light, and it was accompanied by a clockwork-driven rotating set of screens that produced a much brighter light. The old foghorn was replaced with an even louder, compressed-air diaphone in 1914.

In 1919, after serving as keeper of the Discovery Island Lighthouse for twenty-three years, Mary Ann Croft (then fifty-four) applied for a pension. She was told that Ottawa had cancelled light keepers' pensions in 1892. Having nothing to retire on, Mary Ann had no option but to keep working, and she did so for another thirteen years. Not to be defeated by Ottawa's indifference, nor blind to the certain abject poverty that loomed ahead. Mary Ann started working with the rum-runners during Prohibition, relaying messages among them, strategically stationed between the American-patrolled waters of Admiralty Inlet and Canada's Georgia Strait.

By the time Mary Ann formally retired at sixty-seven, in 1932, with an accumulated thirty-six years of service on Discovery Island, she had hidden away enough illicit cash to rent a room in Victoria's Marine Chapel, pension be damned. By then, however, mounting pressure from light keepers across the country had forced Ottawa to restore their superannuation. Mary Ann was presented with an extra $43 per month and a special ceremony for her long years of service. Was the Queen of the Rum-Runners, as she came to be called, ever investigated for her nefarious activities? The police would not say.

In 1918, Captain Ernest Geoffrey Beaumont had bought sixty-five hectares on the southern part of Discovery Island. He built a house for himself and his wife and became an island fixture for the next fifty years. After building a sailboat that he named *Discovery Isle*, Beaumont gained a reputation for hitting every submerged rock in the area—several times. In 1950, his sailing companion, Robert Gale, drowned after *Discovery Isle* struck a reef in Enterprise Channel. In 1967, at age ninety-two, Captain Beaumont died, but not before he willed his land to the provincial government. It would become the Discovery Island Marine Provincial Park. In 1997, the lighthouse was de-staffed and the light automated. By 2004, even the foghorn was gone.

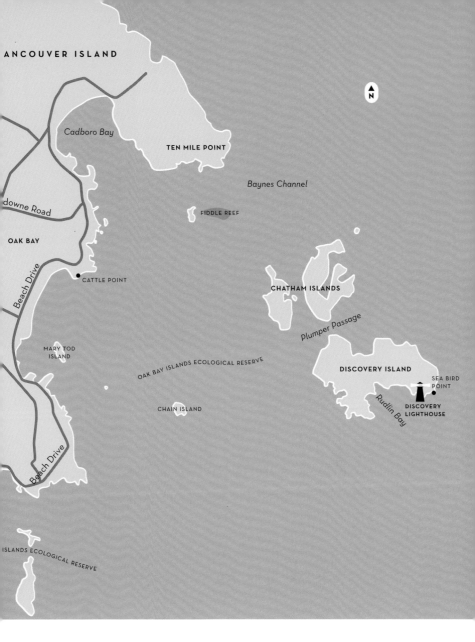

VANCOUVER ISLAND

Cadboro Bay

TEN MILE POINT

Baynes Channel

FIDDLE REEF

downe Road

OAK BAY

Beach Drive

CATTLE POINT

CHATHAM ISLANDS

Plumper Passage

MARY TOD
ISLAND

OAK BAY ISLANDS ECOLOGICAL RESERVE

DISCOVERY ISLAND

SEA BIRD
POINT

Rudlin Bay

DISCOVERY
LIGHTHOUSE

CHAIN ISLAND

Beach Drive

ISLANDS ECOLOGICAL RESERVE

N

6 FIDDLE REEF

LAT 48°25′45.6″ N, **LONG** 123°17′02.1″ W

ACCESSIBILITY ❷ Still Easy

GETTING THERE   The Fiddle Reef Lighthouse is no more, but its stone pier and present beacon are worth paddling or sailing around, if only to marvel that such a fragment of rock, which is barely dry at high tide, could house a succession of light keepers and their families from 1898 to 1958.

There's a handy boat-launch ramp located at Cattle Point, in the Uplands neighbourhood of Victoria's Oak Bay. The stub of the stone pier of the Fiddle Reef Lighthouse is readily visible from there and is less than half a kilometre away, just beyond Tod Rock. It's the perfect spot to launch your kayak for a short jaunt around the kelp-covered reef. Sea lions, pilot whales, and harbour seals are not uncommon at certain times of the year, and among the kelp beds and rock edges of the reef, there's a plethora of sea life from starfish to rock cod. On a

▲ *A blood starfish in the intertidal.*

calm summer's day, it's a safe, easy adventure and good training for further lighthouse-spotting trips, farther afield. Do, however, bring a chart and tide tables along. Make it a circle trip and visit the Oak Bay Marina for a beer and a snack after you're done.

THE WEIRD   In its day, the Fiddle Reef Lighthouse was one of the smallest—if not *the* smallest—lighthouse in all of British Columbia. It was hardly big enough to play a fiddle on. With less than eighteen metres of slippery, kelp-ridden rock to stand upon at low water, going for a walk anywhere on Fiddle Reef at high tide meant staying indoors and hoofing it several times around the main-floor living room of the original tower. At high water, the sea literally lapped at its door. Going to the bathroom meant crossing a wooden walkway to the boathouse and sitting on a holed plank inches above the sea.

The entrance to Baynes Channel is often met with an abrupt change in wind and sea conditions. Mariners call this change a "tide wind." Strangely, "The 'tide-wind' increases when the real wind-strength and tidal flow are opposed, and decreases when wind

▲ *Juanita's home at low tide in the 1950s. At high tide, the ramp is covered completely.* CITY OF VANCOUVER ARCHIVES

and stream are in the same direction. In cases where a sailboat is running with wind and stream of equal strength, in the same direction, it is possible to be becalmed."[46]

Knowing exactly where you were in Oak Bay in such conditions was critical, and the Fiddle Reef Lighthouse, from the last days of sail to the time of GPS, played an important role.

DESIGN AND CONSTRUCTION Fiddle Reef is barely a kilometre off Oak Bay's Willows Beach, in the middle of reef-and-islet-infested Oak Bay, at the southern tip of Vancouver Island. The Fiddle Reef Lighthouse was built in 1898, at the heyday of lighthouse construction on the west coast. The largest islands in the Oak Bay archipelago are Chatham and Discovery Islands. There is a lighthouse at Sea Bird Point on larger Discovery Island that guides ships from the Strait of Juan de Fuca into Haro Strait and the Georgia Strait. Yet, smaller ships often chose the inside of Chatham and Discovery Islands, using Plumper Passage and Baynes Channel as a shortcut to Haro Strait. The Fiddle Reef Lighthouse helped guide mariners through this dangerous inshore maze.

The original whitewashed, pepper-pot-shaped tower stood nine metres above the small rock outcropping on which it stands. The original lamp gallery was painted black, and the focal plane of its beacon was fifteen metres above mean low water. The tower, which also contained the keeper's residence, was built on a square stone foundation fixed to the reef. Beside it, anchored directly to the bedrock, was a boathouse, a launching ramp, and a tank for the coal oil that powered the light. Food and supplies had to be ferried over from Oak Bay by the light keeper in his longboat. Surprisingly, despite its precarious position, the whole structure of the Fiddle Reef light station lasted sixty years and brought nothing but enchantment to the keeper's children, who never felt confined.

THE KEEPERS Juanita (Swanson) Dulong, daughter of light keeper Art Swanson, remembered growing up on Fiddle Reef as a young girl in the 1950s:

> It was around springtime when we first stepped ashore at our new home. As in most early stations there was no phone, electricity, or modern plumbing. Coal oil lamps were our lighting, as well as in the lamp-room. The prism was a beauty and rested on a bath of mercury. I know; I found the little silver balls fascinating. "Never touch that," I was told. But oh my, I was tempted. Lamps, especially the chimneys, were regularly polished with newspaper and vinegar . . .
>
> The boathouse-bathroom often had a surprise, especially at high-tide, or during big storms. "Bottoms" needed to be quick to avoid an ice-cold bidet. Through the "hole" I once saw a huge octopus and a cormorant "flying" under water.

I seem to remember a small fridge and cook-stove, which may have been oil. Baths were taken in a galvanized wash-tub . . . Quarters were small; my bedroom was just an angle (a turning), in the upstairs hallway. The lamp-room was directly above me and I could watch my father's feet as he went up to check the light. Birds were attracted to the light; sometime I even heard them hit. It still breaks my heart.

On one of Dad's grocery trips, a storm came up while he was away. Spray was breaking over the tower. Mom hoped Dad had stayed over in Oak Bay, but she went out [into the storm] often with binoculars. That night I saw something new. It rose up on a long neck, maybe two or three feet out of the water, the light reflected in its yellow-green eyes. It was Cadborosaurus! [the legendary sea serpent of nearby Cadboro Bay].[47]

Little Juanita could not have imagined a more wonderful place to live. Her home at Fiddle Reef was dismantled in 1958 and replaced with a round, automated seven-metre beacon with a quick-flashing (once per second) white or red light. The beacon is all that is left of the light station, and it is off-limits. Yet, seeing Fiddle Reef now, close up from a boat or kayak, will remind you that at one time it was a well-loved family home. What is left is also a graphic reminder that delight and magic have little to do with physical limitations.

VANCOUVER ISLAND

Cadboro Bay

TEN MILE POINT

Baynes Channel

ansdowne Road

JEMMY
JONES
ISLAND

FIDDLE REEF
LIGHTHOUSE

OAK BAY

Beach Drive

CATTLE POINT

CHATHAM ISLANDS

Plumper Passage

MARY TOD
ISLAND

DISCOVERY ISLAND

CHAIN ISLAND

Beach Drive

Mayor Channel

Enterprize Channel

L ISLANDS ECOLOGICAL RESERVE

N

7

EAST POINT

LAT 48°47′ N, **LONG** 123°03′ W
ACCESSIBILITY ❷ Still Easy

GETTING THERE   A day trip to explore the East Point Lighthouse,
its surrounding park, and the other sights of Saturna Island is
as simple as a ferry ride from either Tsawwassen or Swartz Bay.
From the terminal at Lyall Harbour, follow East Point Road
up the hill, past the Lighthouse Pub. With its varying dips and
turns, follow it to Winter Cove Road. Turn right and continue
heading south along East Point to its extreme southeastern tip,
veering onto Tumbo Channel Road for the last little bit. Voilà—
East Point Lighthouse.

The adventure to East Point is a perfect day trip for cyclists.
The route is flat (save a few bumps) all the way to the lighthouse.
Yet, it also has the added bonus of a wonderful side trip—a real ath-
letic grunt—up Mount Warburton Pike. The views from the top of

this peak will take your breath away. If you're staying on Saturna, Boot Cove has a great B&B (call ahead to make reservations). Be sure to bike over to Winter Cove and watch the tidal flow roar through Boat Passage. At the cove's mouth, you'll see the remains of the schooner *Robertson II* on Minx Reef, reminding you that oceans have high and low tides, and that lighthouses do warn the unwary. Finish the day, while waiting for your ferry, over a beer in the Lighthouse Pub and plan your next tourist-free bicycle adventure to yet another compelling light station. Active Pass Lighthouse on Mayne Island is just as easy and close by.

THE WEIRD   On March 2, 1888, the Victoria *Daily Colonist* carried the following advertisement:

> From Ship *John Rosenfeld*
> **BEST VANCOUVER LUMP COAL**
> At Janion's Wharf at
> $5.00 PER TON.
> Bring your own wagon and see it weighed, or
> have it delivered to any part of the city.
> In bags.
> $5.75 PER TON.
> Send orders at once.[48]

Two years earlier, on February 19, 1886, the 2,268-ton sailing ship *John Rosenfeld* was caught in the fierce currents that sweep around the point where Plumper Sound and Haro Strait merge with Georgia Strait. The ship bumped over Boiling Reef and was grounded on East Point. As the tide fell, its back broke and it was declared salvage and put up for auction where it lay. Its hold was full of coal.

The auction went well, and auctioneers Davis and Co. of Victoria quickly sold *John Rosenfeld*'s rigging, fittings, and other gear. The coal was another matter. The ship carried four thousand tons of it, and it lay loose in her bilges. Word of the ship's

▲ *A rare steel tower replacement for the original lighthouse at East Point.*

grounding quickly spread among Saturna Island residents, and soon they were helping themselves to the coal until the salvagers arrived, posting a guard. For islanders, the coal was as valuable as stolen cases of whisky, so the disappearance of some wet coal became a game of avoiding detection. At stake was the rascals' knowledge that what remained of winter, for them at least, could be very cozy indeed. A year later, the underwriters had amassed what was left of the cargo and were selling it in Victoria at bargain prices. Attempts to apprehend the warm, silent, and smiling culprits dissipated like smoke up a chimney. Very droll indeed.

THE NAME Saturna Island is named after the Spanish naval schooner *Santa Saturnina,* which in May 1791 was commanded by José María Narvàez. He and Lieutenant Francisco de Eliza of the *San Carlos* had been ordered from their Spanish base at Nootka to explore the channels to the northeast of the Strait of Juan de Fuca. Sailing in convoy as an expedition, Narvàez and Eliza discovered one particularly large opening they named Gran Canal de Nuestra Señora del Rosario la Marinera—which later became known as

Georgia Strait. Narvàez went on to explore most of the strait alone, as Eliza developed scurvy and returned with his ship to Nootka.

In 1792, Dionisio Galiano in the *Sutil* and Cayetano Valdés in the *Mexicana,* acting on orders from their commandant, Juan Francisco de la Bodega y Quadra, at Nootka, just beat the arrival of George Vancouver in his *Chatham* and *Discovery* into Georgia Strait. On June 22, 1792, the three met off Point Grey and jointly circumnavigated Vancouver Island in the friendly spirit of eighteenth-century rationalism. Initially the island was named "Quadra's and Vancouver's Island," and Vancouver objected to the deletion of Quadra's name, but the Nootka Sound Conventions (1790–94) changed all that.

East Point is at the extreme eastern end of Saturna Island, which itself is the southernmost island of the Gulf Island chain. Because of its geographic position and the long, hooked taper of its tip, the tidal streams appear to boil (hence the name Boiling Reef) around East Point at up to five knots. The flow is further increased as the point lies at the confluence of Georgia Strait, Plumper Sound, and Boundary Pass. Ships passing too close to East Point are in a very dangerous situation.

Two Coast Salish peoples—the Tsawout and the Tseycum First Nations—have lived on Saturna Island for centuries. They called their island home *Tekteksen*, or "Long Nose," due to the hooked shape of the long point at its eastern tip. Today, they hold reserve rights to lands near Fiddler's Cove on the island.

DESIGN AND CONSTRUCTION In 1885, Vancouver had just become incorporated. The would-be city already had a planned townsite, electricity, and the promise of a transcontinental railway terminal. It was poised to boom, and people and goods flooded in, many by ship from San Francisco and beyond. Yet, getting there was problematic. Once past Victoria, vessels left the Strait of Juan de Fuca and turned north into Haro Strait, then east through Boundary Pass, following the Canada–US border until

▲ *The Saturna Island community's response to the loss of their lighthouse.*

making the turn into Georgia Strait towards Vancouver. If fog or storms obscured East Point, ships like the *John Rosenfeld* too often came to grief. Mariners had been lobbying for a lighthouse long before the ship's wreck.

In 1885, Canada set aside money for a lighthouse at East Point but didn't get around to building it until 1888. The $6,000 structure would be similar to others: a square wooden keeper's dwelling with a roof-mounted lamp cupola and gallery. The rotating white light would flash every half-minute and had a focal plane some forty metres above low water. At the same time, a similar light station was under construction on Patos Island, just over the border on the American side of Boundary Pass. Now that there was finally a safe entrance to Georgia Strait, Vancouver boomed.

THE KEEPERS The first keeper at East Point Lighthouse was John Wick from Victoria. But he remained only for a year. James Georgeson, and then his son Peter, took over and ran the station for over fifty-two years. James was the brother of Henry Georgeson, the legendary keeper at Active Pass. Henry would win even more

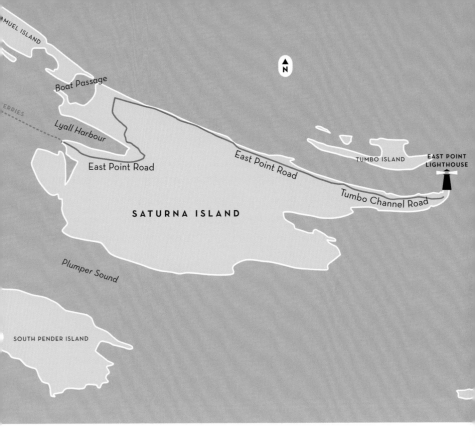

favour when a brush fire broke out at East Point while James was away. Henry hightailed it over from his Active Pass post and put out the fire minutes before it consumed the new station. Both James and Henry spent a fair bit of time away from their respective lighthouses—Henry on his farm on Mayne Island, and James venturing across Georgia Strait to New Westminster for supplies. Although the Department of Marine formally chastised them both for leaving their posts, Ottawa's respect for them never diminished.

Peter Georgeson took over East Point station after his father had a stroke in 1909. When Peter retired some thirty years later, he claimed "that his father, uncle, brother, son, nephew, and two grand-nephews, were all lightkeepers."[49]

In 1939, after repeated demands by marine pilots and towing companies, Ottawa installed an acetylene-powered foghorn alarm building at East Point, which emitted a single piercing whistle every half-minute. Its duration was too short to be of any real worth, especially in stormy, high-wind conditions. It was replaced with a longer, lower, compressed-air diaphone, a Canadian invention, in 1959.

In 1967, according to Donald Graham, the original weather-beaten keeper's house and light tower "were torn down and replaced by a modern dwelling and steel tower."[50] Steel skeletal open towers are a rarity on this coast, are cheaper to build and are readily adaptable to varying height requirements and able to survive the wind and weather extremes sometimes suffered on the inner coast as well as by the reinforced-concrete structures of earlier times. Its fabricated sectional structure has six integrated open platforms with connecting flights of stairs, and its modern airport-beacon light was first used for marine purposes atop the new East Point tower. The light station was de-staffed completely in 1996.

The Saturna Island Heritage Committee turned the fog-horn building into an interpretive centre for the East Point Light Station, and during the summer months it is staffed by knowledgeable island volunteers.

"On May 25, 2013, the Honorable Peter Kent, Canada's Environment Minister and Minister responsible for Parks Canada announced the designation of the first two heritage lighthouses in British Columbia under the Heritage Lighthouse Protection Act."[51] East Point Lighthouse on Saturna Island and Fisgard Light in Colwood gained much-needed public attention. More designations followed.

Much to the dismay of Saturna Island residents, the old lighthouse was torn down in 1967. It was replaced with a new house and skeleton steel tower. But Canada's public wanted more.

JOHN WALLS

8

ACTIVE PASS

LAT 48°52′24.5″ N, **LONG** 123°17′29.5″ W

ACCESSIBILITY ❷ Still Easy

GETTING THERE The Active Pass Lighthouse is probably British Columbia's most frequently viewed coastal light station; tens of thousands of ferry passengers see it each year on the BC Ferries Tsawwassen–Swartz Bay run. The site of the station, with Mount Baker set against Georgia Strait, is stunning and a fitting symbol of BC's maritime history. The view alone has inspired many hopeful lighthouse explorers to get serious.

Visiting the Active Pass Lighthouse up close is quite easy. By car or, better yet, by bicycle, take the Gulf Islands ferry (from either Swartz Bay or Tsawwassen) to Village Bay, Mayne Island. Follow along Village Bay Road to Miners Bay. Along the route, visit historical St. Mary Magdalene Anglican Church, built in 1897. Miners Bay is a great stop for a latte or lunch at Springwater

▲ *A "spirit class" BC Ferry entering Active Pass. Note Mount Baker in the background.* JOHN WALLS

Lodge, which has food and an outdoor deck overlooking the pass. The nearby museum houses the former Miners Bay gaol, so prospectors during their layover certainly had a good time of it. Museum volunteers will fill you in on all the colourful details of Scotty Georgeson's life. A side trip to Dinner Bay, up the hill south of Village Bay Ferry Terminal, is the Japanese Garden, commemorating Japanese-Canadian settlers on Mayne Island who were displaced and interned to the BC Interior after 1941.

There are craft shops and a great new-and-used bookshop at the Fernhill Centre just up from Miners Bay. Doubling back to Springwater, Georgina Point Road will take you directly to the Heritage Park and Lighthouse. It's a delightful, open site—a great place for taking pictures or waving at passing ferry passengers, many of whom are envious of your actually *being* at the lighthouse.

THE WEIRD In August 1881, William Collinson, a Mayne Island homesteader, found an English penny under a stone at Georgina

▲ *The old winch used for hauling the station longboat above the high-tide line.*
JOHN WALLS

Point. Beside it lay a rusty rigging knife that once belonged to a sailor. Collinson noted that the coin was dated 1784. It was known that a boat party under the direction of Captain George Vancouver stayed in this vicinity on the night of June 12, 1792.[52]

THE NAME Archaeological evidence reveals that Coast Salish peoples lived at the narrows they called *S,ktat* in Active Pass for over three thousand years. A settlement and midden at Montague Harbour on nearby Galiano Island dates from 5,000 BCE.

Even at slack tide, Active Pass is too long to be completely free of dangerous tidal currents. At high tide, eddies, fierce standing waves, and hidden reefs make it extremely hazardous for most small craft. For sailboats without auxiliary power, using the pass was out of the question. Yet, gold fever makes people do strange things. In 1858, would-be prospectors from Victoria regularly rowed through the pass in small boats. Most stopped overnight at Miners Bay in the middle of the pass. The next day, largely hungover, they tackled the

▲ *Information and commemorative plaques embellish the site.*

long, fickle crossing of Georgia Strait heading for the mouth of the Fraser River, dreaming obsessively still of Eldorado.

They came in hordes, mostly from America, and their numbers threatened the sober sovereignty of the Crown colony of Vancouver Island. Paddlewheel steamers brought them to Victoria from San Francisco or Seattle. One such ship, USS *Active,* which later became a US government revenue vessel, first transited the pass in 1855, giving it its name.[53]

Georgina Point is named after Georgina Seymour, daughter of Rear Admiral George Seymour, commander of the Royal Navy Pacific Station in Esquimalt from 1844 to 1846.

DESIGN AND CONSTRUCTION Even though short-lived, the Fraser River Gold Rush of 1858 did prompt further exploration of British Columbia's Interior. That first stampede gave way to the

Cariboo Gold Rush of 1860, which triggered the Omineca find of 1869 and the Cassiar bonanza of the 1870s. All this activity steadily increased steamship traffic through Active Pass, which was the shortest marine route between Victoria and Vancouver. Repeated calls for a lighthouse and foghorn soon began.

In 1885, the federal Department of Marine built a light keeper's dwelling at Georgina Point on Mayne Island with a small red lamp gallery attached to its gable peak. Placed at the entry of the channel leading from Georgia Strait, between Mayne and Galiano Islands, the lighthouse allowed for the establishment of a regular ferry service between Swartz Bay and Tsawwassen.

A steam foghorn replaced the original fog bell in 1892, and a white petroleum-vapour lamp, which floated in a tub of liquid mercury, replaced the old wick lamp in 1910. In 1940, the original keeper's house was replaced with a larger wooden two-storey dwelling, and again, a red lamp gallery was placed, albeit higher, on its roof.

Finally, in 1969, an eleven-metre white applecore-design light tower was built on the site, separate from the keeper's house. Its red lantern gallery, at seventeen metres high, housed a white light that flashed every ten seconds. Yet the new lighthouse operated for only twenty years. In 1997, the Active Pass Lighthouse was de-staffed and its light automated.

In 2006, the property was transferred to the Gulf Islands National Park Reserve, and although the tower is now closed, the lighthouse, outbuildings, and grounds have been declared a National Historic Site and refurbished to welcome visitors. There is a parking lot, picnic tables, and information kiosks.

THE KEEPERS Henry "Scotty" Georgeson must have had light keeping in his genes, because not only did he remain at Active Pass for thirty-six years, but he also established a family dynasty of light keepers who carried on in the service long after he retired.

Henry was born on the Shetland Islands. With a limited education he went fishing and soon came to know the hard life the North Atlantic could inflict upon Shetland residents. Henry left Scotland at fourteen to work on the sailing ships, and throughout the 1850s he made voyages to Australia and China. In 1859, Scotty jumped ship in San Francisco and, with thousands of others, headed north to the Cariboo. For a time, he operated a roadhouse near Barkerville, but in 1863, he sold his interest for $2,500. He moved to Galiano Island, pre-empted land, and for five years he farmed, fished, and built boats. In 1868, his marine experience got him the job on the Sandheads Lightship at the mouth of the Fraser River.[54]

Scotty Georgeson was hired for the light keeper's job on Mayne Island before the station was finished, and he lit its light for the first time on June 10, 1885. Known for his dedication and attention to detail, he judiciously rang the initial fog bell and later maintained and operated the diesel air compressor for the diaphones through the ever-present fog. He wound the lamp-rotating mechanism every three hours, twenty-four hours a day; trimmed the wick of the coal-oil lantern daily; cleaned the new lamp's prisms and reflectors; and rigorously kept a logbook, which became the standard for all light keepers for years to come. His log was so thorough that on October 13, 1918, when the CPR passenger steamer *Princess Adelaide* ran up onto the rocks in front of the Active Pass Lighthouse in a pea-soup fog, its captain tried to blame Georgeson, claiming he neglected to sound the horn. Scotty's log told a different story. The captain was dismissed.

Scotty's son, George, became a light keeper as did his brother, James, who manned the East Point Lighthouse from 1889 to 1921. James's sons, Peter and Henry, also grew up to become long-time light keepers on the BC coast.

Although Scotty Georgeson was the consummate keeper of the Active Pass Lighthouse, ships still foundered in Active Pass. In March 1915, the tug *Alberni* got caught in its own cable while trying to free another tug, *Sea Lion*, from Collinson Reef. *Alberni* capsized and sank halfway through the pass.

More recently—in the days of radar and other electronic aids to navigation—two BC Ferries came to grief in Active Pass. On August 2, 1970, BC Ferries' MS *Queen of Victoria* "collided with the

◀ *Note the solar panel for the new light.*

Russian freighter *Sergey Yesenin* in Active Pass. Three people were killed including a 31 year old Ann Hammond and her 7 month old son, Peter." Hammond's husband, George, witnessed their disappearance under a crumple of cars amidships, just as the freighter struck. An inquiry determined that the freighter was in the passage when he shouldn't have been, and the captain was forced to pay damages.[55]

On August 9, 1979, BC Ferries' *Queen of Alberni* struck Collinson Reef in Active Pass, just after 7:00 a.m. on a falling tide. Passengers and crew were evacuated from the ferry, and no one was injured. The falling tide caused the ship to list thirty degrees, which resulted in vehicles and semi-trailer trucks sliding into each other and prompting fear of a gas leak and consequent explosion. An inquiry found that the likely cause was a sports-fishing boat obstructing the ferry's right-of-way and the ferry's "lack of manoeuvrability at high speed."[56]

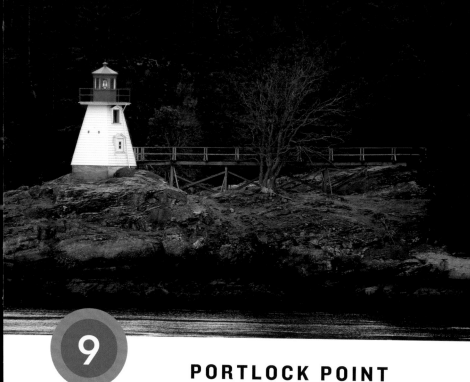

PORTLOCK POINT

LAT 48°51'27" N, **LONG** 123°20'43.9" W

ACCESSIBILITY ❸ Moderate

GETTING THERE Because there is no public ferry to Prevost Island, you must get there by private boat. Don't let that stop you, because with a kayak, the world opens up before you. Ruckle Provincial Park, at the southeastern tip of nearby Salt Spring Island, has glorious, full-facility waterfront camping spots. The campground overlooks Swanson Passage and would make the perfect base camp for a couple of days' exploration of Prevost Island and its lighthouse. The short crossing of Captain Passage (about one nautical mile) through the Channel Islands to the southwestern shore of Prevost Island is easy, though you might incur some BC Ferries wash. Exploring Prevost Island's Ellen Bay and Diver Bay en route to the lighthouse is an added bonus.

Another way of getting to Prevost Island is to kayak to James Bay on the island's northwestern tip. James Bay is also part of the Gulf Islands National Park Reserve and has ten rudimentary camping spots (pit toilets, no open fires), which could readily suffice. However, there are no public trails on the island, and so from James Bay you must kayak down the Trincomali Channel side of the island, through the Charles Rocks, to the Portlock Point Lighthouse at its southeastern tip.

Still another way is to sail over to Prevost and anchor in Glenthorne Passage or Annette Inlet. I much prefer the latter; it's completely protected from the weather and has great holding ground. Although it's limited to sailboats that draw less than 1.5 metres, and there's a tricky rock at its entrance to navigate around. Once you are in Annette Inlet, you'll never want to leave.

While you are on Prevost Island, explore Selby Cove and the meadows beyond Annette Creek. At the lighthouse, try the walkway across the rocks to the tower, see if you can find the charred remnants of James Heanski's house, and *do* wave at the passing ferries.

◀ *Volatile lamp oil caused the March 1, 1964, explosion.*
CITY OF VANCOUVER ARCHIVES

THE WEIRD Prevost Island is one of the most beautiful of the Gulf Islands. It is also the largest, completely underdeveloped piece of property in the island chain. Its pastoral meadows, thick, first-growth forests, and numerous long inlets forge a landscape so enchanting that it inspired both hunting and music. In the late nineteenth century, several prominent Victoria businessmen created a private hunting club on Prevost, gleefully shooting the same deer they had imported to the island. Later, one of the daughters of Hubert de Burgh, a descendant of Irish aristocrat Digby de Burgh, who bought the island outright in the 1920s, grew up on Prevost Island. She responded to a different natural impulse and became a concert pianist.

THE NAME Prevost Island is named after Captain James Charles Prevost, commander of HMS *Satellite,* which the Royal Navy had posted to its base in Esquimalt from 1857 to 1860. Prevost did well for himself. He was born in 1810, in the ancient village of Bedhampton, Hampshire, which overlooks the sea and Portsmouth Harbour. Prevost joined the Royal Navy at thirteen, became a lieutenant at twenty-five, and commander of his own ship ten years later. In Esquimalt, he married the daughter of the base commander, Rear Admiral Fairfax Moresby. In 1856, Prevost was appointed first commissioner in the settlement of the San Juan Island boundary dispute between the British Empire and the United States.

Portlock Point is named after Admiral Moresby's flagship HMS *Portlock.*[57] Coast Salish peoples called Prevost Island *Xwes'hwum* ("place having fur seals"), and evidence found among the island middens suggests that it has been inhabited for at least two thousand years.[58]

DESIGN AND CONSTRUCTION Prevost Island is surrounded by Trincomali Channel, Swanson Channel, and Captain Passage and is smack in the middle of the southern Gulf Islands. From the Fraser River Gold Rush in 1858, to Vancouver's burgeoning growth in the 1880s, this marine highway between Victoria to the Lower Mainland became the prime course for the ferries of the Canadian Pacific Navigation Company, numerous freighters, marine-towing companies, and later BC Ferries.

But there was a problem. Directly before Active Pass and northeast of Prevost Island lies menacing Enterprise Reef and other rocks, which are awash at high tide. It was believed that lights on the reef and on Portlock Point itself would alert mariners when to make that critical turn north into Trincomali Channel and safely into Active Pass.

There were already wooden-stake lights on the reef and at Portlock Point, but in 1895 federal lighthouse agent James Gaudin wanted something more substantial. George Frost of Nanaimo won the contract for $870 and built a fifteen-metre pyramidal wooden tower, with attached lean-to kitchen and living space, on Portlock Point. Its fixed white, seventh-order dioptric light (with a prism-magnified, refracted lens) had a focal plane of twenty-two metres. The lamp had rotating baffles, producing a red sector light, which warned ships coming to or from Active Pass that they had strayed into the path of Enterprise Reef. The keeper was given the added task of operating a hand-driven fog bell which rang out its warning to ships converging on the Pass "in the thick" from its many surrounding channels.

THE KEEPERS   When Portlock Point Lighthouse was completed in 1896, the patrician members of the Prevost Island hunting club believed that the first keeper of the Portlock Point light should be one of their own, thereby maintaining the privacy, dignity, and privilege to which they had become accustomed. However, once they discovered the minuscule annual salary that Ottawa was prepared to pay for the job, they scoffed. The first keeper of the Portlock Point Lighthouse would be an outsider.

▲ *BC Ferry in Swanson Channel*

John Richardson kept the light at Portlock Point for nine years, from 1896 to 1905. His successor, W.J. Gillespie, stayed only six. When George Watson became the keeper in 1911, his annual salary amounted to only $460. In a letter to his MP, Watson argued that his salary was completely inadequate for a man supporting a wife and two sons. Hearing nothing, Watson ignored his immediate superiors and wrote directly to the Minister of Marine and Fisheries.

Watson's letter was passed on to the department's Victoria agent, who was enraged by the keeper's defiance. The agent shot back, saying that if Watson didn't like the job, he knew where he could put it. But this spirited farm boy didn't bend, and in the end he received a $90 increase in his yearly wage. Watson became the spokesman for other light keepers in British Columbia who felt cheated and debased by Ottawa's tight-fisted treatment.

But Watson's fight with Ottawa wasn't finished. Over the next few years he argued that working conditions at most light stations were impossible for one man; rotating lamp mechanisms, automatic fog bells, and vapour lights needed attention twenty-four hours per day. It was unconscionable, he wrote, that the costs incurred for mechanical repairs, cordwood for heating the tower in winter, and medical costs for keepers and their families all had to come from their meagre wage.

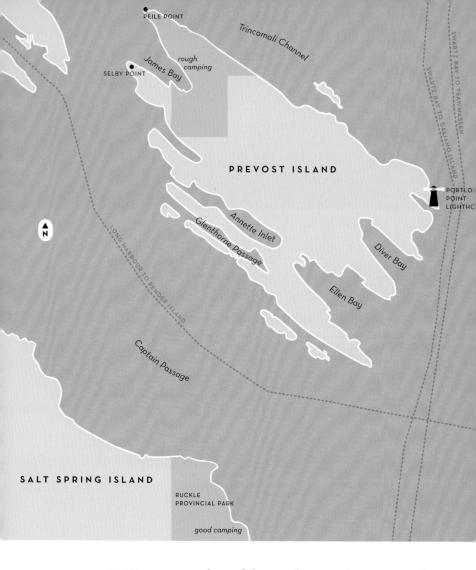

PEILE POINT

Trincomali Channel

SWARTZ BAY TO TSAWWASSEN

SWARTZ BAY TO GALIANO ISLAND

rough
camping

James Bay

SELBY POINT

PREVOST ISLAND

PORTLO
POINT
LIGHTHC

N

Annette Inlet

Glenthorne Passage

Diver Bay

Ellen Bay

LONG HARBOUR TO PENDER ISLAND

Captain Passage

SALT SPRING ISLAND

RUCKLE
PROVINCIAL PARK

good camping

In 1924, one year short of the mandatory retirement age of seventy, George Watson suffered serious internal injuries when a 189-litre oil drum fell on him. It took four days and the incalculable waving delight of many innocent passengers on Canadian Pacific Navigation Company ferries to notice that his inverted ensign was being flown at half-mast. In the end, it was a Cowichan man in a fishing boat who saw the distress signal. He didn't know what it was; he just happened to see the upturned flag and surmised the bedridden keeper simply wanted to buy a fish.[59] Later that year, Watson was declared unfit to work and given a retirement annuity one-third his regular annual wage.

In 1949, a new detached keeper's house was built at Portlock Point. By then, radio communications, medical care, and correspondence schooling for the keepers' children had become available.

On the evening of March 1, 1964, an explosion and fire, heard and seen by many on the surrounding islands, engulfed the keeper's house at Portlock Point. Although passing ferries responded, as did the coast guard, it was too late for keeper James Heanski. His body was found in the ashes beside fragments of a kerosene lamp, which investigators later believed had caused the accident.

In 1964, the Portlock Point Lighthouse was de-staffed. A new, smaller, automated tower, along with a helipad, replaced the original in 1967. In 2006, the lighthouse became the property of Parks Canada and added to the Gulf Islands National Park Reserve.

▲ *Throughout the Gulf Islands the bald eagle population seems to be thriving.*

10

PORLIER PASS

LAT 49°01′44″ N, **LONG** 123°35′07″ W

ACCESSIBILITY ❸ Moderate

GETTING THERE There is a daily (car) ferry service from Tsawwassen or Swartz Bay to Sturdies Bay on Galiano Island, and the trip to see the beacon at Race Point and the light at Virago Point is well worth it. The view across the strait from Race Point is amazing.

Leave the car at the terminal and make it a day trip by bicycle. The sixteen-kilometre bike ride up the long spine of the island to Dionisio Point Provincial Park is full of surprises. Visit Montague Harbour and walk the Penelakut midden beach. After your coffee at Sturdies Bay, if you happen to be there on a Saturday in July or August, visit the Galiano Museum located in Aunt Di's Cottage in Lions' Park. Forget seeing the lights from the seat of a kayak— it's far too dangerous. Instead, enjoy your exploration of Galiano Island more safely from the seat of a bike.

THE WEIRD Denice Goudie, granddaughter of Henry Edward Brown, the keeper of Porlier Pass Lighthouse from 1949 to 1965, often visited the station with her mother to see her grandfather. Recalling her memories of those stays, she said:

> For some, the sound of the foghorn is sad and forlorn, to me that sound is one of safety as I recall waking and knowing, no matter what, all was well as Grandad was taking care of everything as he pumped away on that ancient, hand-driven foghorn.[60]

THE NAME Porlier Pass, where the lights stand, separates Valdes Island from Galiano Island, two of the northern Gulf Islands. The Pass was named by José María Narvàez, captain of the *Santa Saturnina* and co-commander (with Francisco de Eliza) of the Spanish expedition that explored the inner waters of Georgia Strait in 1791. Narvàez named this fast-flowing waterway Boca de Porlier. *Boca* literally means "mouth." *Porlier* is more difficult to source in that it is a family name and could possibly stand for the Spanish admiral Rosendo Porlier y Asteguieta, who rose quickly through the ranks of the Spanish Navy and later tried to defend Cádiz from Nelson's attack of 1797. Narvàez possibly knew him or respected his abilities. When Galiano and Valdés explored the Gulf waters a year later, Boca de Porlier had already been marked on the charts they used.

The Penelakut First Nation people had summer fishing camps on Galiano Island for centuries. *Penelakut* literally means "log buried on the beach," referring to the beachfront aspect of their summer lodgings. The Penelakut ranged from Chemainus on Vancouver Island to Valdes, Galiano, Thetis, and Penelakut Islands.

DESIGN AND CONSTRUCTION There are two routes through the Gulf Islands large enough for steamships: Active Pass and, farther north, Porlier Pass. The tidal flow through Active Pass is strong, but being the wider of the two, it is safer. However, Porlier Pass was almost adjacent to the early-twentieth-century coal and logging ports of Crofton and Chemainus, and in the commercial shipping language of the day, time was money. But Porlier Pass is short, narrow, and lined with rocks and reefs at its edges, and it has extremely strong tidal flows. The currents in Porlier Pass often run up to ten knots. With its multidirectional flows, over-falls, dangerous eddies, and huge standing waves, Porlier Pass, even at slack tide, demands respect.

That respect was often flaunted by mariners despite the warnings in the pilot books of the day. Virago Rock was discovered the hard way when the side-paddlewheel steamer HMS *Virago* struck it in 1853. The six-hundred-meter-long steamer *Del Norte* was carried onto a submerged reef in Porlier Pass in 1868, and in 1893 the German steamer *Romulus* hit its namesake rock in the middle of the pass in 1893. It took lobbying from mariners, captains of industry, and the head of the Esquimalt and Nanaimo Railway to get the federal government to agree to build a lighthouse at Porlier Pass. If private enterprise couldn't be stopped by the forces of nature, government intervention could, at least, be goaded into reducing corporate losses.

The federal lighthouse agent in Victoria, James Gaudin, recommended that Vancouver Island business demands be met. They were for a set of two range lights. These lights, when aligned one behind the other, would give steamships a safe compass bearing to follow as they headed into the pass from Georgia Strait. The light facing the strait was on an exposed bare-rock spur known as Race Point. It sported a white-painted seven-metre-high square wooden tower with an octagonal lamp cupola and gallery. The rear range light, half a kilometre away across Lighthouse Bay on Virago Point, faced the inner Gulf Islands of Thetis and Penelakut (then called Kuper) with Chemainus on Vancouver Island just beyond. It was a white-painted pyramidal wooden tower ten metres high and had a

▲ *Pelagic cormorants leave their mark.*

flared top to receive a six-sided cupola and gallery. Originally, both lamps were continuous burning, though Virago's lamp was magnified by prisms (dioptric), and Race Point's lamp was brightened by reflecting mirrors (catoptric). The rear light (Virago), therefore, was slightly higher and the brighter of the two. Neither tower had an attached dwelling. The lamps were lit on November 15, 1902.

THE KEEPERS One of James Gaudin's selling points to the federal government was that the Porlier lights needed no keeper's residence because his choice for the first keeper was a Penelakut man who lived on the island. But the area's MP, Ralph Smith, insisted that the position be filled by a Caucasian applicant, thus angering and alienating the local First Nations for years to come.

In 1902, Francis Logan Allison got the job. With no accommodation provided by the lighthouse service, and a monthly salary of $30, he lived in the bunkhouse left by the contractors who built the Virago Point Lighthouse. In 1907, he married Mathilda Georgeson, the granddaughter of Henry "Scotty" Georgeson, keeper of the

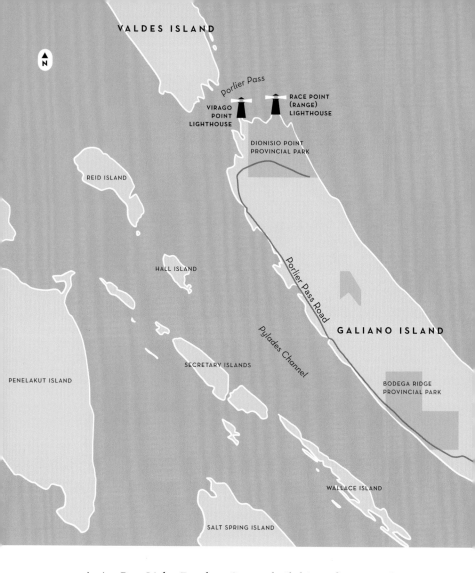

Active Pass Light. For that, Ottawa built him a four-room house and supplied the station with a freshwater cistern and a hand-pumped foghorn. Mathilda soon bore Francis two daughters, Devina and Frances, and as they grew up, the girls helped their father keep the lights at Race Point and Virago with such dedication that he won commendations from shipping corporations and fishermen alike. Devina would write of him, "My father was not a religious man, but he was a good man with a heart of gold."[61]

Trouble came when local Aboriginals who perceived Francis as the one who had cheated them out of a job began complaining. They wrote to Ottawa repeatedly, stating that he drank and was abusive towards them, and they demanded that he be transferred. Ottawa didn't investigate but warned the light keeper about future complaints.

In 1915, Mathilda Allison died. Seven years later, Francis married Elizabeth Gear and became the stepfather of a fifteen-year-old boy. But the marriage didn't last. In 1929, Elizabeth charged him with assault. Francis Logan Allison was hauled into court and forced to pay her $40 a month in separation allowance. Drink, inflation, and a staggeringly low wage turned the light keeper into an embarrassment for the Department of Marine and Fisheries, and steps were taken to have him removed—to little avail.

None of Francis Allison's personal troubles would cast doubt on his well-known, exemplary performance as a light keeper. In the early years, he had banged a hollow tin drum in the fog when Ottawa first denied Porlier Pass a proper foghorn. He had pulled umpteen grateful survivors from the swift waters of Porlier Pass in the 1920s. He put his job on the line in 1927, when he appealed to Ottawa for a siren foghorn. In the early 1930s, he fed hungry Natives. In 1934, "He rescued Mr. C.D. Cotton, a Vancouver insurance broker, whose party was swamped in the pass."[62] Francis Logan Allison might have suffered the slings and arrows of outrageous personal misfortune, but at Porlier Pass, he was absolutely essential. In 1942, at age seventy-six, after forty years of service, Allison retired.

In 1966, the front range light on Race Point was torn down and replaced with a cylindrical beacon. Later that year, the Virago Point Light was de-staffed, and parts of the old tower are now held in the Galiano Museum. Francis Allison's daughters, Devina and Frances, both married light keepers who also served their time at Porlier Pass.

ENTRANCE ISLAND

LAT 49° 12′ 34″ N, **LONG** 123° 48′ 25″ W

ACCESSIBILITY 4 Hard

GETTING THERE It is possible to circle Entrance Island by kayak or other small boat, though the trip demands some open-water experience in small craft. There are fine views of Entrance Island from the BC Ferries Horseshoe Bay–Departure Bay (Vancouver to Nanaimo) run. However, viewing the lighthouse close up from Gabriola Island would make a terrific day trip. Take the Gabriola Island ferry and from Gabriola Terminal follow North Road, turning left at Taylor Bay Road, which soon becomes Berry Point Road, which takes you to a viewpoint.

While on Gabriola, reward yourself with a visit to some finely incised Aboriginal petroglyphs. "Church Site" contains a number of fabulous glyphs of fish, mythic serpents, and human figures, while "Cliff Site" reveals a fecund female figure and her family. At the head of Degnen Bay is a glyph of a killer whale, best seen at low tide. Ask before you go glyph hunting, and be sure to read Mary and Ted Bentley's fine book, *Gabriola: Petroglyph Island*, before you go.[63]

Visit Silva Bay for a beer and a snack and then peruse the art gallery and bookshop at nearby Page's Resort and Marina. A paved road encircles Gabriola Island, so it would make a fine, easy day trip from Nanaimo by bicycle.

THE WEIRD Climate change and a keen-eyed keeper made meteorological history on Entrance Island on the morning of February 17, 2011. Entrance Island light keeper Glenn Borgens witnessed *five* water spouts, all descending to the sea from the inky-black clouds above Georgia Strait very near to the lighthouse. Immediately, Borgens notified the coast guard in Nanaimo of this rare phenomenon. They, in turn, notified the weather office. Tornadoes, even over water, are to be avoided.[64]

THE NAME Entrance Island is little more than a four-hectare rock outcropping some nine metres above high water, about a kilometre off Gabriola Island in Georgia Strait. It is located at the entrance to Nanaimo's Departure Bay. The Snuneyuxw peoples lived on Gabriola Island and the surrounding area for centuries and fished among the Flat Top Islands and in the tidal streams of Gabriola Passage, Dodd Narrows, and Northumberland Channel. Along the way they developed a substantial culture. Gabriola Island itself is rich in Indigenous petroglyphs, remnants of a large Snuneyuxw village at False Narrows during the mid-Marpole period, over two thousand years ago.

In 1791, the Spanish named the northern point of Gabriola nearest Entrance Island Punta de Gaviota, or "Cape Seagull." Seagulls, too, knew of the perennial whereabouts of salmon. It's believed that smallpox began to wipe out the summer inhabitants on the island even before the dreaded epidemic struck the Indigenous population on Vancouver Island in 1862.

DESIGN AND CONSTRUCTION Coal deposits around Nanaimo were confirmed as early as 1852 when Hudson's Bay Company clerk Joseph MacKay took possession of the find for James Douglas. In 1862, the HBC sold its coal interests at Wintuhuysen (later known as Colville), and by 1872, Robert Dunsmuir's Wellington mines were shipping out over one hundred tons per day. All this traffic needed a lighthouse to warn mariners of the rocks and reefs near Entrance Island at the entrance to Nanaimo Harbour. A Montreal contractor named Louis Baker was hired to build a lighthouse and keeper's dwelling on the tiny, exposed outcropping in 1875.

Full of ego and bluster, Baker swore he'd complete the job in three months. By February 1876, with the work little more than half done, Baker absconded with the money. Workers and suppliers were left destitute, so the Department of Marine hired James Gordon to oversee its completion. He, too, disappeared with the government's money two months later.

Finally in April 1876, the job was done. Entrance Island Lighthouse stood as a square white wooden tower almost a hundred metres high with a small light keeper's house attached. Its first light

▼ *The self-sufficient Entrance Island Light Station. Note the ladder for the long-boat crew.*

was really a combination of six separate oil-lamps which merged through a lens into a single beam. The resulting lamp wasn't that bright, and in 1891 a fifth-order dioptric lamp replaced the original, sporting a sectored beam that shone red when vessels strayed too close to dangerous Gabriola Reef. In 1905, the lamp was replaced again with an even brighter fourth-order beam, and in 1921 the whole heavy apparatus was rotated in a mercury bath to facilitate a distinguishable flashing sequence. The old steam foghorn was replaced with a gasoline-driven, air-compressed diaphone in 1921.

In 1970 the old tower was replaced with a 112-metre cylindrical reinforced-concrete structure, which remains today.

THE KEEPERS Murder and mayhem? The evasion and cunning that plagued the construction years of Entrance Island Lighthouse weren't limited to its builders. Entrance Island light keeper M.G. Clark turned his job into a money-making racket. Clark and his wife were both disinclined to do much light keeping, and so they bought a farm on nearby Gabriola Island. Clark hired assistants and demanded, as part of their job description, that they must not only keep the lighthouse in good order but also work on his farm. The mean-spirited taskmaster either underpaid them or refused them a salary altogether, simply pocketing what they were due for himself. One such assistant, Hugh Breslin, found out about Clark's tight-fisted ways all too soon.

"When I got there," Breslin wrote, "I was forced to feed the chickens, dig the garden and clean the house for his wife."[65] Once that was done, he was ordered to row over and tend the light. After two months Breslin quit. Then things got really strange.

In November 1910 Breslin's successor, another assistant keeper, disappeared from Entrance Island completely. Presumably he drowned in the course of his duties, but suspicions soon turned upon Clark himself. Without a body, however, Clark remained free, becoming little more than a scary, if frustrating, suspect.

In December 1910, Clark demanded a pension and early retirement from Entrance Island. He cited failing eyesight as the reason. The federal lighthouse agent posted in Victoria paid him a surprise visit one day and found him spry, vigorous, and reading a newspaper. Clark backtracked cautiously.[66]

In 1911, Clark hired Allen Pope and his wife as assistant keepers at Entrance Island. Suddenly, Mrs. Pope found herself doing the laundry for both couples, cleaning the farmhouse, and tending the chickens while her husband fed the pigs, tilled the land, and took on all the duties of a full-fledged light keeper. Made of stronger stuff than her husband, Mrs. Pope complained to Ottawa, citing all the details and noting that Clark seldom worked at all. Feeling that something was in the wind, Clark summarily fired the Popes, ostensibly for being late to work. Clark himself was finally fired from the service in 1913.

Little changed. W.E. Morrisey replaced Clark as the new keeper at Entrance Island in 1914. Though Morrisey didn't run a farm, he, too, expected his assistant keepers, Edwin and Bertha Perdue, to do most of the work. Bertha wrote to the federal lighthouse agent in Victoria. The bureaucratic agent responded with a typical, terse dictum that "they were wholly under the orders of the lightkeeper."[67] It would take years for Ottawa to specify the workload of assistant keepers. Morrisey himself remained at Entrance Island only to the end of 1914.

Clark and Morrisey were certainly not the norm at Entrance Island Lighthouse, but they did bring into focus some of the early weaknesses of the official strict hierarchy in Canada's light stations.

In 1995, word got out that Entrance Island Lighthouse might lose its keeper and become yet another de-staffed and automated station on the BC coast. Hundreds of kayakers formed a human life preserver around the island, claiming the cost-cutting move would only end up costing lives. The public outcry forced officials in Ottawa to back off, and Entrance Island Lighthouse remains manned, for the moment.

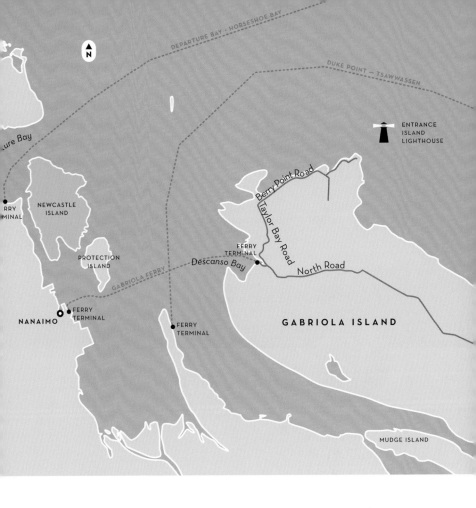

During the sunny afternoon of August 25, 2014, nine lives were saved from certain drowning in the cold waters of Georgia Strait when a pleasure craft involved in a fishing excursion swamped and overturned approximately one nautical mile off Entrance Island. Light keeper Tony Greenall saw the sluggish craft sinking lower in the water and immediately raced to the scene in his own boat. After the rescue, a coast guard official reported that everyone was cold but alive. The Entrance Island keeper wrote, "It's very important to have eyes out there."[68]

12

BALLENAS ISLANDS

LAT 49°21′02″ N, **LONG** 124°09′36″ W

ACCESSIBILITY ❹ Hard

GETTING THERE A trip over to Ballenas Island requires a boat. Ocean kayakers should be experienced and travel in pairs or groups. The difficulty is in the crossing. It's approximately two nautical miles, and the best route is from the marina at Schooner Cove. Along the way you can see the Winchelsea Islands in all their glory. However, as the islands used to be used as a torpedo-tracking station, landing there may still be prohibited. There are Royal Canadian Navy buoys in the cove west of the southernmost island and other protected coves (if you are exploring in a larger boat), which might serve you well in an emergency or severe change of weather. Pay very close attention to the afternoon winds, which blow down Georgia Strait on sunny summer afternoons.

THE WEIRD Ingenious to the last, island light keepers are not easily daunted by the elements or by loneliness, and one anonymous Ballenas Islands keeper simply stared down the devil of desperation with defiance. The windswept islands are little more than two thirty-six-hectare scraggy islets connected by a stepping-stone rock of sorts. They have few trees and are pockmarked with hollows full of scrub-grass and bush chaparral. Nevertheless, this enterprising light keeper, during his early days on the islands, found enough grass in the hollows to be trimmed into the greens of a seven-hole golf course. Sand traps weren't a problem, but overshooting the holes, thereby committing his balls to the deep, was always a frustration.[69]

THE NAME The Ballenas Islands lie north of Nanaimo, just off the eastern edge of Vancouver Island. At the mouth of a long inlet called Nanoose Bay are the Winchelsea Islands, two of the nineteen islands that make up the Ballenas–Winchelsea Archipelago. These islands dot the western side of Georgia Strait from Nanoose Bay to Parksville. The Ballenas are the most seawards islands of this archipelago.

In 1791, José María Narvàez, commander of the *Santa Saturnina,* saw a pod of whales off the island group, consequently naming them Islas de las Ballenas. That sighting convinced him that the Gran Canal de Nuestra Señora del Rosario la Marinera (Georgia Strait) had another opening to the Pacific Ocean beyond its southern beginnings at the Strait of Juan de Fuca. In 1792, George Vancouver proved Narvàez right. Exploring the Georgia Strait, he continued sailing north, leaving the largest landmass to his port side, eventually entering Queen Charlotte Sound and the Pacific Ocean. The huge landmass was indeed completely surrounded by water, and it came to be named Vancouver Island.

DESIGN AND CONSTRUCTION By 1899, the federal Department of Marine and Fisheries had on its books a series of light stations planned to guide mariners safely past the northern Gulf Island and beyond, through the maze of islands north of Desolation Sound. In 1900, an eight-metre-high square and tapered wood tower and foghorn was planned for North Ballenas, but bureaucratic bungling had it built in the wrong place, "atop a high knoll in the centre of the south island."[70] That position proved to be useless for navigators, in that bearings taken from the middle of an island (which then would become a line of position), could not save a ship from the dangers that lay beneath the sea at both ends.

Strangely, a shed for a hand-pumped bellows foghorn was built at the tip of the northern island in 1908. Perhaps Ottawa's lighthouse service knew something about the placement of the light tower, but they weren't letting on.

THE KEEPERS Charles Drummond would have known, and he would have told all and sundry. The owner of the islands in the 1880s, he drowned in a skiff while rowing back from Nanaimo in 1889. He had already willed the islands to his Aboriginal wife, Maggie, but Ottawa chose to ignore her rights of ownership and placed the lighthouse on South Ballenas Island, squarely in her midst.

The first light keeper on Ballenas was a German immigrant named William Brown (a.k.a. Wilhelm Betatit). Brown married Maggie Drummond (Charles Drummond's widow), but theirs was a turbulent union, and in 1905 the lighthouse agent in Victoria discovered that William had been imprisoned in Nanaimo for domestic violence. Brown was eventually committed to the newly built Woodlands mental hospital in New Westminster. Until William's nephew arrived from Germany to become Ballenas's second keeper, Maggie, ran the light. She was not acknowledged nor paid by the government for her interim service.

Maggie moved in with Brown's nephew (also called Wilhelm) soon after he arrived from Germany. They lived for a time on South Ballenas, which demanded a daily row over to service the

▲ *West Ballenas from the air. Note the Winchelsea Islands and Nanoose Bay (Schooner Cove) at the top right.*

compressed-air engine in the foghorn shed. In 1910, in league with her relatives, Maggie called her second husband "unfit," and had him tossed out. In 1912, sensing chaos, the federal government had the original tower pulled down and relocated to the tip of North Ballenas, next to the original foghorn shed. By then a new foghorn, boat ramp, boathouse, and windlass made the station's facilities at least complete.[71]

In 1912, Arthur Gurney arrived with his family to become the islands' next keeper. Brown may have been mad, and his nephew useless, but Gurney turned out to be a consummate conniving pest in the eyes of the federal service. At the root of Gurney's (and other keepers') disquiet were the unbelievably low wages the federal government paid to its light keepers. Getting nowhere in his repeated demands for a livable wage, Gurney enlisted in World War I, leaving his wife, Anna, and their three children to look after the station. For a time, the federal lighthouse service simply looked the other way.

Gurney returned from the war with a commissioned officer's pension, and along with his wages he was able to live well

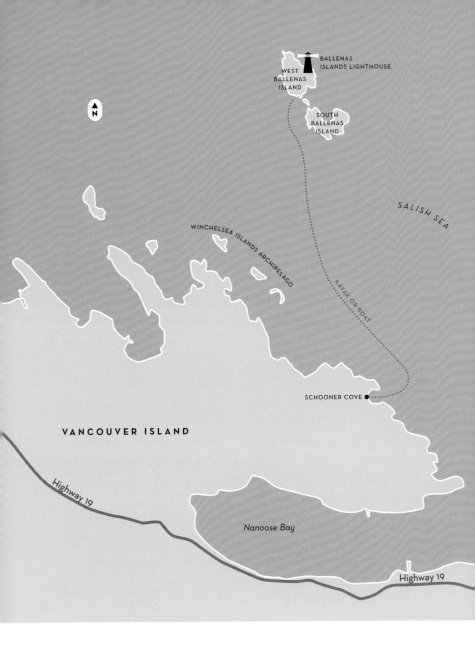

BALLENAS
ISLANDS LIGHTHOUSE

WEST
BALLENAS
ISLAND

SOUTH
BALLENAS
ISLAND

N

SALISH SEA

WINCHELSEA ISLANDS ARCHIPELAGO

KAYAK OR BOAT

SCHOONER COVE

VANCOUVER ISLAND

Highway 19

Nanoose Bay

Highway 19

and send his children off to boarding school.[72] In this, Gurney was unique—in 1920, the government still wasn't providing correspondence-school support or wages to the keepers' wives in order to give station children an education. Gurney continued to pester the lighthouse service about working conditions and wages, and in 1920 he was transferred to Active Pass Lighthouse on Mayne Island.

For the last keepers of the Ballenas Islands Lighthouse, Rita and Richard Wood (1994–96), life was different. The station was just twenty minutes from Parksville by powerboat, and the keepers' battles with Ottawa seemed to be over. By the 1990s, regular tours of duty and scheduled helicopter support replaced months of isolation. Yet, Richard knew that the golden era of the light keeper was over. "All the gadgets in the world can't replace the eyes and ears of a human," he told author Lynn Tanod. "Besides," he continued, lifting a glass of homemade blackberry wine, "if we want to get a little bit crazy, there's no one to wag their fingers at us."[73]

Ottawa did wag its finger, however, and on September 1, 1996, the Ballenas Islands Lighthouse was de-staffed. In 1998, the Land Conservancy of British Columbia purchased South Winchelsea Island for $595,000. Because the islands are rich in biodiversity and provided habitat for several species of sea mammal, the conservancy planned to return the entire Ballenas–Winchelsea Archipelago to their original state. The Island Trust proposed a similar plan specific to the two Ballenas Islands.[74]

Yet, as of 2014, South Ballenas is still privately owned and for sale with the asking price of $1,450,000. Worse, active development of the island is being encouraged.[75]

13

SISTERS ISLETS

LAT 49°29'10" N, **LONG** 124°26'06" W

ACCESSIBILITY ➍ Hard

GETTING THERE   A flyover is definitely the best way to see the Sisters. From that vantage point, which reveals the absolute limitations of its size and its unprotected exposure to the weather, gives the place the perspective and respect it deserves. Although the crossing from False Bay on Lasqueti Isand to the Sisters is short, the weather there is often substantially different from weather in other parts of the gulf. Perhaps the anomaly is due to the Qualicum winds, which blow east across Georgia Strait from Parksville or Qualicum Beach, interfering with the usual northwesterlies that blow down the strait in summer. The Sisters is also largely in open water, and its open fetch from the north can produce large waves.

If you are setting out for a closer look by boat or kayak from False Bay, don't go alone. Only sailors and paddlers with plenty of experience should attempt this trip.

THE WEIRD If you think being sentenced to solitary confinement on Alcatraz Island in San Francisco Bay is something fierce, try living alone on the Sisters. This minuscule, barren, rocky outcropping smack in the middle of Georgia Strait saw five light keepers in its first six years. They fled the place due to its vulnerability to the seas, the complete lack of space, and the overwhelming sense of isolation.

THE NAME The Sisters is a cluster of absolutely barren crags, recognized on a marine chart as two dots—two rocks, two "sisters," of almost identical size. They are located some sixteen kilometres northwest of the Ballenas Islands in the centre of Georgia Strait. One-third the way from False Bay at the western side of Lasqueti Island to St. John's Point, on southeastern Hornby Island, the Sisters stand alone. The rocks are little more than two nautical miles off Lasqueti Island itself. However, they might as well be off the coast of Africa, in that the short crossing from Lasqueti is often fraught with contrary winds and big seas.

DESIGN AND CONSTRUCTION It was the ship owners' complaints for more navigational aids on Georgia Strait at the start of the 1898 Klondike Gold Rush that prompted Ottawa to consider a proper lighthouse for the Sisters Islets. Perhaps it was a dose of paranoia; perhaps it was the startling look of the two black specks on the charts that made federal lighthouse agent James Gaudin exclaim to his boss that the Sisters "is the first that should be lit."[76] Either way, it was a poor choice. Ships heading north up Georgia Strait from Victoria, Vancouver, or Seattle were more likely to bear over to the western side of the strait to pick up the Ballenas light, and then proceed to where they could see the range lights of Chrome Island off

Denman, running down them a bit before turning north again for Sabine Channel and the Inside Passage. Ballenas was much more visible. However, the decision was made to construct a "proper" light station on the Sisters, and in 1898 work began.

There was already a day beacon that had been on the islets since 1897; the plan at the time was for something more substantial that would include a light tower and a dwelling to entice an unknowing keeper and perhaps his family. George Frost of Nanaimo won the $3,200 contract and built a raised masonry foundation upon which would sit a rectangular wooden two-storey house. Potable water would be piped from its roof to a cistern within the foundation, while the light tower protruded from one of its gables, some ten metres above the sea. The lamp, a seventh-order light, shone dimly out into the gloom. Notices for a keeper were soon distributed, and the fun began.

THE KEEPERS In December 1898, a bachelor named Ronald McNeill first lit the light. He quit eight months later in August 1899, claiming he hadn't seen hide nor hair of anyone in eight months. In September 1899, Harry Higgins and his wife arrived. She lasted six months; Harry claimed it was the fog bell in the attic that drove her nuts. Harry himself bailed out in February 1901. Alfred Jeffries made it to October 1901. He blamed his wife, claiming she was sick. Benjamin Blanshard stayed for two years with a wife and young daughter—a considerable feat in that the child couldn't venture outside for a little outdoor recreation in windy and inclement weather fearing she'd be swept into oblivion by a rogue wave. Moreover, when it rained, the place leaked like a sieve. W.C. Ferneyhough hacked it only for five months from July to November 1904.

In 1907, Ottawa decided a diaphone foghorn was required, and wiser, older Benjamin Blanshard sensed an increase in salary was in the wind and reapplied. His salary rose from $300 to $800 per year, but he was required to find and pay for an assistant

▲ *How much things have changed!*

keeper to maintain the machinery and run the compressed-air diaphone out of his own wages. He hired his wife. It worked, and the Blanshards and their children stayed for another two years, quitting finally in May 1910.[77]

When Walter Buss rowed over to Lasqueti Island on November 19, 1912, to visit his dentist, a fishing boat was shipwrecked in a storm on the deserted islet. Buss had already asked the Department of Marine for a salary increase but was ignored, so his decision to leave his post and have his teeth fixed didn't elicit any guilt towards his tight-fisted federal employer. When Buss heard that the rescued fishermen had told Ottawa of the abandoned station, he just grinned. His letter of resignation was dated September 28, 1912—three weeks before the shipwreck. Ottawa had to shoulder its own negligence and Buss was too clever to be jacked around yet again.[78]

The jacking around continued, however. From attempting to charge keepers for mail delivery to refusing to respond to material requests in a timely manner, the Department of Marine failed

to consider the human element of life on the Sisters. They knew families with children wouldn't go near the place; they also knew that the bachelor lifestyle of the men they were able to employ would relegate the place to vermin-infested ruin. If storms continually splintered the longboats, demolished the boathouses, and tore away at the structure of the keeper's dwelling, it was Ottawa's neglect of those who served at the Sisters that finally brought the station to its knees.

In 1967, Ottawa was forced to tear down what was left of earlier structures and construct a reinforced-concrete tower, a new foghorn building, and new living quarters replete with electricity and a helipad. Keepers would work for the next twenty-five years in guaranteed short-term postings of two weeks on and two weeks off. In 1996, the Sisters Lighthouse was de-staffed completely, its buildings boarded up and closed. The site is off limits to the public today, and it is being considered for demolition due to vandalism. Before it's gone forever, lighthouse aficionados ought to get close enough to snap that elusive picture.

▲ *A once truly magnificent structure.*

14

CHROME ISLAND

LAT 49°28′20″ N, **LONG** 124°41′5″ W

ACCESSIBILITY ❸ Moderate

GETTING THERE   If you are car-topping a kayak or carrying bicycles, drive north on Island Highway 19 and take the Buckley Bay exit to the Denman Island ferry. On Denman, follow traffic heading for Hornby Island and continue on through Boyle Point Provincial Park. There's a spectacular overlook to Chrome Island at the end.

The best way is to take bikes over to Hornby Island and cycle to Ford Cove. There's a marina there with kayak rental facilities. From there, it's a short trip across Lambert Channel to Chrome Island. While you are on Hornby Island, stay in the tenting ground (or a B&B), and visit the spectacular cliffs of Helliwell Provincial Park. Then, go for a swim at Tribune Bay, the warmest waters in all of Georgia Strait. Chrome, Denman, and Hornby Islands are jewels in the Salish Sea.

THE WEIRD Tom Piercy brought his wife and his ten children with him when he first arrived. Together, Tom and his wife raised and home-schooled each of the children and gave them a life to be envied by the young everywhere. That is, all except one. Young Harvey Piercy, age eight, found a strange-looking metal object near the lighthouse one day, and in trying to examine it with a rock, the rusty blasting cap exploded. Harvey's thumb was gone and his hand mangled as his father rowed him over to Denman Island. There, he instructed the lad to hold his reddened and bandaged hand high and find the island doctor. Tom left his son on the beach and immediately returned to his vacated post at the station. Young Harvey set out through the bush alone, found the doctor, and was fine. His father, however, grew a few white hairs.

THE NAME Royal Navy surveyors charting Georgia Strait in detail for Admiralty charts in the 1860s are said to have named this 1.2-hectare island Yellow Island, which is probably how the lighthouse keepers began calling it Yellow Rock. The names were no doubt inspired by the buff-coloured lichen that grew on the limestone rock-faces and glowed golden-yellow in certain afternoon-light conditions. However, the name was changed in 1940 to Chrome Island to avoid confusion (especially in wartime) with another Yellow Island much farther north in Discovery Passage.[79]

K'ómoks (Comox) peoples occupied the eastern side of Vancouver Island and the northern Gulf Islands for thousands of years. They called their territory *kw'umalha,* meaning "plentiful and wealthy"—and it was. Deer lived in the woods, and oysters, salmon, seals, sea lions, and whales thrived in the channels of Georgia Strait. The remnants of wooden stakes protruding from the mud flats near Comox are remains of the extensive weirs used by First Nations people to trap fish, and stand as testament to the rich bounty of their ancient homeland.[80]

DESIGN AND CONSTRUCTION At the same time that tens of thousands of would-be prospectors travelling by steamer from Victoria and San Francisco flocked to the unnamed creeks of the Klondike, immigration to North America from Europe began in earnest. And all these ships needed coal. New coal deposits in Cumberland and other mines on eastern Vancouver Island helped fill this need and was shipped worldwide from Union Bay. Sensing exponential growth, company officials ten years earlier had demanded navigational aids for vessels heading into the wharves in Baynes Sound. Canada's Department of Marine responded by establishing lighthouses throughout Georgia Strait and the Inside Passage. Within a ten-year period at the end of the nineteenth century, light stations were constructed at Saturna Island, Ballenas Islands, Merry Island, the Sisters Islets, Cape Mudge, and Chrome Island.[81]

In 1890, J.A. Brittancourt of Nanaimo was awarded the $4,000 contract. First he had to blast away enough rock to create a level space to build a square wooden dwelling on the southern tip of Chrome Island with a lamp-tower gallery and railing protruding

▼ *Protected petroglyph on Chrome Island.*

from its roof. The station became operational when the island's first keeper, Tom Piercy, lit the fixed white lamp on December 31, 1891. It wasn't enough.

One dim light shining out through the gloom into Georgia Strait didn't cut it. The southern entrance to Baynes Sound between Denman and Vancouver Islands narrowed considerably, especially at Repulse Point. Mariners wanted range lights to mark a bearing, a line of position so to speak, which when aligned could safely guide ships through the narrows to the deeper, centre waters of the sound. So, in 1898, two towers were built one behind the other on Chrome Island, the southwestern one being higher, at some twenty metres above high water.

It worked until December 17, 1900, when during a fierce winter snowstorm, the steamship *Alpha* drove right up onto the rocks in front of the Chrome Island Lighthouse. The *Alpha* was well known on the Victoria–Alaska run. The steamer was unsuited for northern waters; it was far too underpowered and had too small a rudder to be effective in strong winds. Worse, the *Alpha* had a long history of poor helmsmen as evident by its numerous scrapes along its hull from the Alaska pack ice. The ship was also known to be poorly maintained. Helmsman C. Swanson reported after the grounding that "the steam pumps were useless and no suction could be obtained."[82]

It was said that twenty-six souls locked themselves hand-in-hand to get through the boulders and surf to the shore that dreadful night, and light keeper Doug McDonough fed, warmed, and gave first aid to the survivors. Five others, still on board when the ship broke up, perished.[83]

In 1908, a compressed-air diaphone foghorn was added to the station. In 1922, the old protruding tower was dismantled and replaced by a separate, open, steel-framed tower. That stood until 1989 when the skeleton structure was replaced with a cylindrical reinforced-concrete tower and outbuildings, which remain today.

THE KEEPERS   Schooling was always an issue for the children of Chrome Island light keepers, as it was for the families on other coastal stations right through to the 1960s. John Doney quit his post in disgust in 1913, after he was reprimanded by a federal lighthouse inspector for leaving the station without written permission, in broad daylight to visit to his boys at school on nearby Denman Island.

The Bruton children, three girls and a boy, were home-schooled during the 1960s as they moved with their father's postings on Discovery, Lennard, and Chrome Island Lighthouses. Sharon and Elanie Bruton both remembered their mother, Evelyn, helping them work through their huge correspondence-school packages without financial support from the lighthouse service. This despite the fact that most mothers became home-school teachers out of sheer necessity. In 1961, tired of her husband's poor wages, the Department of Marine's nonsensical regulations, and Ottawa's indifference towards their children's education, Evelyn Bruton and others organized lighthouse mothers up and down the coast and threatened to go on strike if they weren't reimbursed for their active teaching. In 1962, the Department of Marine relented and paid each mother who taught a minimum of four children a stipend of $30 per month in the absence of a proper public educational system. Sharon was nine before she went to a "real" school. When she did, she absolutely excelled.[84]

Through it all, perhaps it was life's other lessons that the self-reliant lighthouse children learned more directly than their urban counterparts did. In 1963, a fisherman brought over the Bruton children's young cousin for a visit and anchored near Yellow Rock, as the locals still called Chrome Island. However, the fisherman suddenly became unwell and sought help from light keeper Jim Bruton. Jim left his post and went to the shore, carrying the ailing fisherman back up to the lighthouse. Then he set out again to tow his anchored boat to a safer position on the lee side of the island, leaving the stricken man in the care of his eldest daughter, Linda.

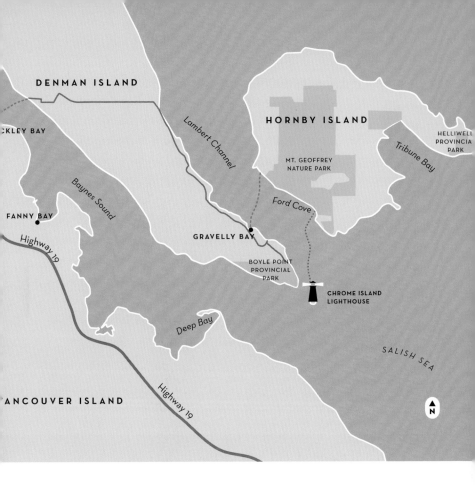

Sadly, the fisherman died in the girl's arms of a massive aneurysm. Linda was just ten years old.[85]

If the exigencies of life and death are more severe to light keepers and their families, their very isolation often put them face to face with other powerful mysteries from an earlier time. Chrome Island is guardian to some amazing Aboriginal petroglyphs thought to be over a thousand years old. More than just "rock art" or "Aboriginal graffiti," as some have called it, these incised stone carvings are evidence of the very origins of literacy.

Research in the last few decades has revealed that while these stone images may be beautiful in themselves, they ought to be seen more "as a form of non-alphabetic literacy."[86] The glyphs range from dream visions to abstract renderings of Indigenous stories and experiences, and they have been shown to contain pre-alphabetic elements such as rings, chevrons, vertical lines, and dots, which should be seen as analogous to the instructions embedded in the icons of, say, our own highway-information signs. In other words, the graphic elements that often accompany so-called artistic petroglyphs are clues as to how they ought to be "read," because they contain widely known and widely distributed symbols concerning Aboriginal cosmology and spirituality. We ought to look at the Chrome Island and other coastal petroglyphs in the same way that we gaze upon ancient Egyptian or pre-Columbian South American hieroglyphs. The problem is, we haven't yet figured out all the "letters."[87] If you see them, treat them with respect; you are standing on wondrous ground.

▼ *The rocky edge of Chrome Island and the yellow lichen, which gave the island its former name, Yellow Rock.*

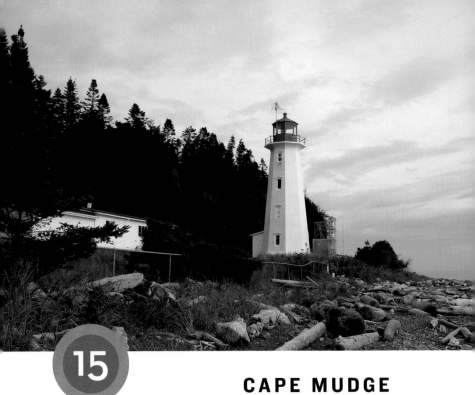

15

CAPE MUDGE

LAT 49°59′52″ N, **LONG** 125°11′42″ W

ACCESSIBILITY ❶ Dead Easy

GETTING THERE Cape Mudge is one of the few island light-houses of southern British Columbia that is readily accessible by automobile and even has a parking lot. Yet a far better way to get a feeling for Quadra Island while visiting the Cape Mudge station is to make it a day trip by bicycle from Campbell River.

Once you arrive in Campbell River, there are plenty of safe parking lots near the ferry to Quadra Island where you can leave your car. Crossing Discovery Passage from Campbell River to Quathiaski Cove on Quadra Island takes only twenty minutes by car ferry. From the ferry terminal at Quathiaski Cove, follow Heriot Bay Road until its junction with Cape Mudge Road. Turn right, then head south veering slightly right along Joyce Road. Continue until you reach Lighthouse Road and turn right again.

Head past the entrance to Tsa-Kwa-Luten Lodge and carry on down the hill to the lighthouse parking lot.

Along the beach in front of the lighthouse is a breathtaking view of Georgia Strait, and carved into the boulders on the foreshore are several significant Indigenous petroglyphs. Pack a lunch in your day-pack. On a shining summer day, a bicycle trip to Quadra Island and the Cape Mudge Lighthouse is a venture you will remember.

THE WEIRD If you drop a glass windowpane on a ceramic tile floor, the shattered result would resemble what happened to BC's inner coastal topography at Cape Mudge, on Quadra Island. Suddenly, the clear, open vastness of southern Georgia Strait becomes a splintered labyrinth of islands through which the whole North Pacific Ocean must surge, twice daily, on its gravitational, push-and-pull roar, to and from the open sea.

THE NAME George Vancouver was only thirty-five years old when he sailed north up Georgia Strait during the summer of 1792, but he'd done more and seen more than most men twice his age. The farther north he sailed, the less he liked the place. In June, he wrote, "Through this very unpleasant navigation we sailed and its appearance was very inhospitable."[88] Vancouver was referring to the myriad waterways and dark, wooded islands of Desolation Sound. Just westwards of them across the narrowing gulf lay the Discovery Islands, an equally huddled and densely set group of small islands and their fast-flowing network of watercourses, which would lead him finally to the northern ocean. Getting through them would be tough, but Vancouver's hunch about the huge landmass on his port side would turn out to be true. Vancouver Island, he would prove, was indeed an island.

Vancouver must have been feeling less desolate in late July 1792, because he named Cape Mudge, the southernmost tip of Quadra Island, after his first lieutenant on HMS *Discovery*, Zachary Mudge. The men had much in common. Vancouver had joined the Royal Navy at age thirteen; Mudge joined at ten. Both rose through the ranks quickly and had the same views towards naval discipline. Both had gained a vast amount of sea experience by the time they were twenty. Both were resolute men, and both readily understood each other.

The We Wai Kai Nation occupied most of the lands near Cape Mudge for centuries. They are a subgroup of the Laich-kwil-tach peoples. Today members of the We Wai Kai Nation's thriving population of over one thousand reside mainly on five reserves, including those at Village Bay, Drew Harbour, and Cape Mudge on Quadra Island and at Quinsam in Campbell River.

DESIGN AND CONSTRUCTION Georgia Strait shallows quickly just before the bedlam of islands (Quadra, Cortes, Redonda, Hernando, Maurelle, Sonora, and the Chained Islands) at the mouth of Discovery Passage. Of the lot, Quadra Island is by far

▼ *The proud tower overseeing the whole of southern Georgia Strait.*

WARNING
FOGHORN
MAY SOUND

the largest island, and for large ships it marks the eastern gate to the only route through this labyrinth north to the Pacific Ocean.

The discovery of gold in the Yukon in 1896 soon led to an unprecedented stampede of hopeful prospectors from America and around the world. Tens of thousands rushed north to the Klondike, to Dawson City and into the vastness of the Yukon Territory between 1897 and 1899, and all needed ships to carry them. Most ship captains preferred to voyage north from San Francisco or Victoria through less violent seas than those of the open Pacific, so most chose the inshore route. With the loss of the USS *Saranac* in Seymour Narrows on June 22, 1875, and American shipping companies clamouring for a lighthouse at the Passage's southern entrance, the American government added their voice to the growing brouhaha. Canada, of course, took notice and jumped at the American government's demands.

It was George Frost of Nanaimo who built the first square wooden two-storey lighthouse and lean-to in 1898. It was cheap, costing just over $1,000, and like many other lighthouses on the coast at this time, its red-painted tower and lamp gallery protruded from the roof some nine metres above the sea. A seventh-order dioptric-lensed lamp (fairly dim) was placed in the gallery and would shine out into southern Georgia Strait for sixteen kilometres. In 1908, the original lamp was replaced with a brighter second-order Fresnel lens unit. It didn't help much.

THE KEEPERS The affable and self-reliant Scotsman John Davidson lit the lamp at Cape Mudge for the first time on September 16, 1898. The post was considered a plum job in that the town of Campbell River was a short row away, and the Davidsons had friends on Quadra Island, especially at nearby Quathiaski Cove. As author Donald Graham notes, when fog spilled into the narrows, or the currents raced north, southbound vessels often anchored near the light, and "local residents rowed out to the

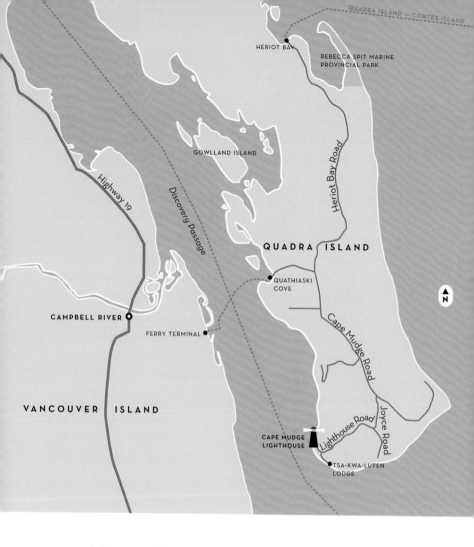

moored ships to trade news and gossip over the rails."[89] Coming from the isolated Sisters Islets light station, the Davidsons often found themselves besieged by visitors. The Davidsons loved it and stayed at Cape Mudge for twenty years.

On the afternoon of January 26, 1911, the SS *Cottage City* missed seeing the Cape Mudge light in a driving snowstorm and ran up onto rocks near the cape. Davidson had been at the shore all day cranking his foghorn, but the steamer was running blind in heavy weather. It drove right onto the inshore rocks. Davidson guided all the passengers and crew safely through the surf, then warmed, fed, and bedded them at the lighthouse until help arrived. Although Ottawa was grateful for the light keeper's actions, they wouldn't pay him for expenses he incurred, nor would they grant him a one-day paid medical leave two years earlier, despite the fact that he hadn't had taken any holidays for eleven years straight. What they did do was install a new, more powerful diaphone— but since Davidson did not have an assistant to maintain the air compressor, this simply increased his workload. Davidson continued to scrap with Ottawa over missing supplies, overwork, poor wages, inflation, and general indifference to the keeper's plight until he left the service in 1918.

His successor, Herbert Smith, was posted to Cape Mudge from the light station at Nootka. He immediately had his wages cut by $300 a year because the fog at his new posting occurred less often than at his previous posting. Go figure.[90]

Cape Mudge suffered from a high turnover of keepers; most were disgruntled by working conditions and poor wages until the station was threatened with closure in 2009. Citizen protests gave the light station a reprieve, and Dennis Johnson remained its keeper until 2014. The lighthouse grounds are open, and although the station is fully electrified and may be unmanned today, there are staff there in spring and summer to answer visitors' questions.

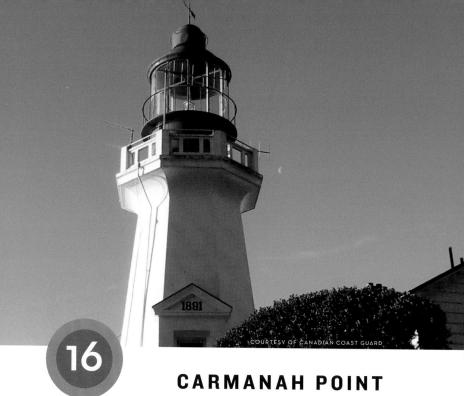

COURTESY OF CANADIAN COAST GUARD

16

CARMANAH POINT

LAT 48°36'43" N, **LONG** 124°55'03" W

ACCESSIBILITY ⑤ Really, Really Hard

GETTING THERE First drive to Bamfield on Vancouver Island's west coast. If you are intent only on seeing the light stations at Cape Beale, Pachena, and Carmanah Point, you ought to consider doing the whole West Coast Trail from north to south. You will need to apply for a provincial park permit (guaranteeing you a spot) early in the season, because numbers doing the trail are strictly controlled. This is a difficult hike, one of the most demanding in the world, and you will need about a week to do it.

Read all the books and carry tide tables and detailed maps of the West Coast Trail. Be careful where you camp along the beach, and note that firewood supplies at Tsusiat Falls are limited, especially during July and August. It's best to do the trail from Bamfield to Port Renfrew, leaving the muddy slog at the southern end until your muscles have hardened. Cape Beale is a bit out of your way at the beginning, but Pachena and Carmanah Point lie directly on your route and can be readily seen from the trail. When I was there last, the light keepers had short trails cut directly to their stations. The keepers I met were most welcoming, but tread lightly as you are on private property. This is an adventure you will remember for a lifetime, but train for it and go fully provisioned.

THE WEIRD   Carmanah Lighthouse was built in the wrong place. In 1790, Sub-Lieutenant Manuel Quimper, captain of the captured British sloop *Princess Royal,* was ordered by the commandant of the Spanish outpost at Nootka to explore the coast to the Strait of Juan de Fuca. He did, and named the highest, most prominent peninsula Bonilla Point ("Bold Point"). In 1792, Commander Jacinto Caamaño charted Quimper's observations. A year later, Vancouver was using Caamaño's charts for his own explorations.[91] In 1846, when the British Admiralty began duplicating Spanish charts in earnest, they placed Bonilla Point on their maps farther north than it should have been. The wrong name was attached to a lower promontory surrounded by shallow water. That misnaming was error number one.

In 1890, a lighthouse was chosen for Bonilla Point, so surveyors and labourers using the incorrect maps dutifully began the job of moving building materials for a tramway up the wrong incline. At the top they found themselves staring south at the intended, but misnamed, higher promontory, the real Bonilla Point. Faced with a long, arduous, corrective slog, the workers said to hell with it and built the lighthouse where they stood, on the lower headland—on Carmanah Point. That was error number two.

THE NAME   Although the name Carmanah sounds like the Spanish name Caamaño, it is really an English similitude of the Ditidaht word *kwaabaaduw7aa7tx*, pronounced "Qua-ma-doa" and meaning "thus far upstream." Walbran noted that it referred to a settlement situated under the promontory's low eastern bluff, which once belonged to a band of Indigenous people known for their ferocity. Their largest village, Whyac, sat at the estuary of the Nitinat River as it pours out of Nitinat Lake into the sea. Sealers, explorers, and British surveyors began using the name Carmanah in the 1860s, and it was picked up by Admiralty map-makers soon after.[92]

DESIGN AND CONSTRUCTION   America had already established a lighthouse at Cape Flattery at the mouth of the Strait of Juan de Fuca in 1857. Captain G. Richards of the Admiralty survey ship HMS *Plumper* argued, in 1860, that a light station should be built opposite the American one on the Vancouver Island shore, marking a safe "gate" to the often fog-bound entrance to the strait. Nothing was done for until 1887, when CPR head W.C. Van Horne stated that Canada's coffers (and CPR profits) would suffer if ships continually stood off the strait waiting for clear weather. Ottawa stirred.

Finally in May 1890, errors and time aside, tenders were invited for the construction of a fourteen-metre square-high wooden tower with an attached light keeper's house and separate fog-alarm building. It was to be located at the western extremity of Carmanah Point. The focal plane of the light shone out into the night from a height of fifty-three metres. By November, the steamers *Maude* and *Douglas* had carried enough lumber to Carmanah Point for contractor George Frost, who had by this time expanded his company and relocated to Victoria, to build a tramway for the heavy wooden joists and substantial cupola and lamp gallery from the beach to the site. W.P. (William) Daykin was transferred to Carmanah Point from Race Rocks Lighthouse and lit the seventh-order dioptric lamp for the first time on September 15, 1891. Its rotating, clockwork apparatus shone out into the gloom for thirty kilometres. Baffles shielded the beam intermittently, producing the effect of three white flashes per minute. The builders did a substantial job at Carmanah Point with the allotted $15,000 because the original lighthouse lasted thirty years.

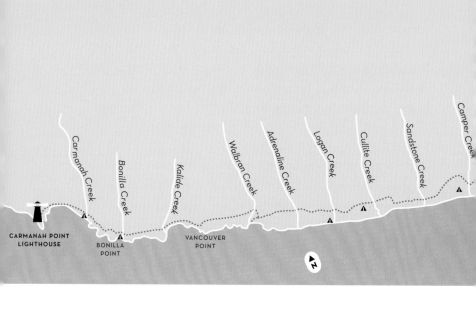

In its early years, Carmanah Point also boasted a high-pitched steam whistle so messages could be sent from ship to shore via Morse code even during frequent, heavy fog. They were then relayed on to Victoria via the landline telegraph cable. It was Daykin who began the practice, initially out of his salary, of caching stores along the telegraph line for shipwreck survivors. During that time, his act of humanity cost him both money and personal grief. On March 13, 1892, the Victoria *Daily Colonist* reported that Daykin "suffered considerably by thieving Indians who have helped themselves to the Government stores."[93]

By 1910, the lamp's brightness had been increased to a fifth-order dioptric-lens unit. The original coal-fired, steam-powered foghorn was also replaced that year with a much more reliable diesel, compressed-air diaphone. But Daykin was not a ready convert to the boasts of modernity. It was said he had a flock of carrier pigeons standing by to do the work of the cable when the hurricane winds of winter blew it from its strung-out perch among the trees.

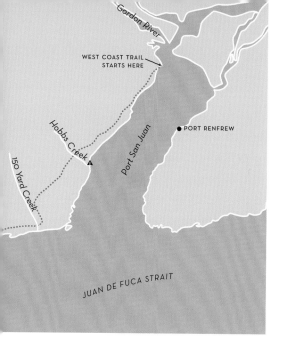

THE KEEPERS W.P. (William) Daykin remained at Carmanah Point for twenty-one years, from 1891 to 1912. He liked his booze, reportedly knocking back a bottle of Scotch a day. His supply line of alcohol became threatened in 1892 because in August the Victoria *Daily Colonist* reported that "the little, black sloop *Edith* along with another vessel [had] been placed under detention by Customs authorities. The *Edith* had been a frequent violator of the law, visiting and trading at West Coast stations while paying scant attention to the formalities of Canada Customs. When Customs agents learned the *Edith* declared nothing they seized the ship and alleged it sailed for the purpose of discharging illegal whiskey."[94] It didn't take long for Daykin to find other illicit suppliers of his drink; and he needed it then more than ever.

In October 1893, his oldest son, Ted, drowned while fishing with a friend at Nitinat Narrows. Scarcely a year later, on September 20, 1894, his youngest son, William, died at age thirteen when he fell to his death from the aerial cable car that served the station to the rocks below the lighthouses. In the early winter of 1906, Daykin's wife, Anna, underwent abdominal surgery in

Victoria. Convalescing at Carmanah Point, she died of infection in April 1907.

Daykin's life as keeper at Carmanah Point was not only full of personal grief; it came latterly with a hefty sense of bitterness towards the Department of Marine and Fisheries. At the outset of his employment, he was promised an annual salary of $1,200, and for that he had to do the following: play nursemaid to a reluctant lamp for nearly two dozen years; wind the clockwork; rotate lamp apparatus every three hours, twenty-four hours a day; feed the fires of the old steam-powered foghorn; maintain the new diesel engine; wrestle coal, lamp oil, and other supplies up the tramway; communicate with passing ships using flag semaphore and Morse code; relay shipping movements and daily weather reports to Victoria via the telegraph; keep the grounds in good order; and maintain a vigil for those in peril at sea. It was said that W.P. Daykin witnessed so many shipwrecks and deaths while on his watch at Carmanah Point Lighthouse that he became the unofficial sexton of the marine graveyard which lay before him.

By 1912—the year he was transferred to McLaughlin Point Light in Victoria—Daykin was fed up arguing for the pay that Ottawa had promised him. In the end, he was increasingly full of invective for his employer, while at the same time he was crippled with arthritis. Some said he suffered with mercury poisoning from the rotating lamp apparatus. He died in 1916.[95]

George Woodley, Daykin's successor, took one look at Carmanah Point and stayed only six weeks. Ironically, Robert Daykin, another of William's sons, succeeded him and remained five years. In 1920, radio phones were installed at the station. In 1922, the original wooden light tower was replaced with an eleven-metre octagonal reinforced-concrete structure, which bore a huge third-order Fresnel-lens lamp. It served until the light was electrified in 1960. The keepers' houses were replaced in 1948 and again in 1957. Carmanah Point Lighthouse is one of the few light stations that remains manned toady.

CARMANAH POINT LIGHTHOUSE stands at the beginning of the aptly named Graveyard of the Pacific. Heavy seas, the set of the tide, the northern flow of the current, the rock-strewn lee shore of its west coast, and the fog made it treacherous for sailing ships and early steamers alike. Hundreds of ships and lives are entombed here on rocks stretching northwards from Carmanah Point to Nootka Sound and beyond.[96] Here are but a few:

Ships wrecked with lives lost:
Sarah (barque), Pachena Point, November 8, 1891—four lost
Michigan (steamer), Pachena, January 20, 1893—one lost
Ivanhoe (schooner), disappeared, September 1894—all lost
Janet Cowen (barque), Klawana, December 31, 1895—ten lost
Cleveland (steam brig), Barkley Sound, December 9, 1897—nine lost
Laura Pike (schooner), Clo-oose, March 4, 1902—all lost
Pass of Melfort (barque), Barkley, December 28, 1905—all lost
Valencia (steamer), Pachena Point, January 22, 1906—126 lost
Soquel (schooner), Seabird Rocks, June 22, 1909—two lost
Renfrew (seiner), Nitinat, November 17, 1918—thirteen lost
Alaskan (steamer), Pachena Point, January 2, 1923—all lost
Varsity (seiner), Pachena, February 9, 1940—four lost
St. Clair (tug), Port San Juan, November 16, 1948—three lost

Ships wrecked with no casualties:
Ericsson (barque), Barkley Sound, November 19, 1892
Eagle (schooner), Barkley Sound, September 11, 1918
Tuscan Prince (freighter), Clayoquot Sound, February 15, 1923
Nika (freighter), Ucluelet, February 15, 1923
Santa Rita (freighter), Clo-oose, February 15, 1923
Robert Lewers (schooner), Pachena, February 23, 1923
Taatjana (freighter), Barkley Sound, February 26, 1924
Raita (schooner), Clo-oose, January 18, 1925
HMCS *Thiepval* (minesweeper), Broken Islands, January 29, 1930
Nereus (freighter), Cape Beale, August 8, 1937
Uzbekistan (freighter), Pachena, April 30, 1943
Liberty Ship (freighter), Tsusiat, June 22, 1944
Glafkos (freighter), Amphitrite Point, January 1, 1962[97]

Even with the upgrade of the telegraph line from Cape Beale to Victoria in 1907, which would become the Dominion Lifesaving Trail, it was the light keepers of the Carmanah Point, Cape Beale, and Pachena Point light stations who were largely responsible for saving the lives of those who made it through the pounding surf to this wild, isolated, and unforgiving shore.

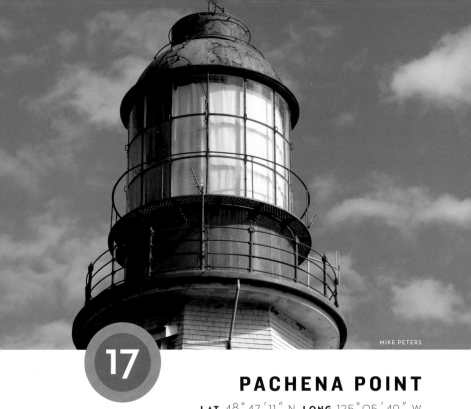

MIKE PETERS

17 PACHENA POINT

LAT 48° 47′ 11″ N, **LONG** 125° 05′ 49″ W

ACCESSIBILITY ❹ Hard

GETTING THERE Bamfield is beautiful, and getting there is easy. Drive north on Highway 19. Beyond Nanaimo, look for Highway 4 west to Port Alberni (Exit 60). Turn left onto the Port Alberni Highway. In Port Alberni, turn left onto Dunbar Street, which becomes Anderson. Turn left and follow the signs for Bamfield. You should be on Franklin River Road. Follow it for forty-six kilometres to Bamfield, and voilà! You are there.

Once in Bamfield, you will see signs pointing to the trailhead and West Coast Trail parking lot. You must apply to do this trip early in the spring, as Parks Canada puts a limit on the number of hikers on the trail at any given time. If you are serious about seeing the Pachena Point Lighthouse, get a West Coast Trail guidebook, or read the copious Internet sources for information on the trail. You are embarking on one of the finest coastal hikes in the world, but you must go prepared.

If a round trip of some twenty kilometres is too much for you in one day, you can camp at Mabens Beach, which is ten kilometres away. At low tide, the rocks, tide pools, and sea-grass beds here are truly spectacular. Prepare as you would for a wilderness hike of several days. Don't forget to carry fresh water.

THE WEIRD Things changed quickly on the west coast of Vancouver Island after the 1906 tragedy of the steamship *Valencia*. It missed the Strait of Juan de Fuca and steamed onto the rocks near Pachena Point. Several attempts to get a line ashore failed, and the reports of 126 passengers facing a horrific death in the surf, only forty-five metres from shore, so unnerved and angered British Columbia's coastal population that Ottawa began the construction of a lighthouse at the point as soon as the 1906 inquest on the disaster was laid to rest.

Was it haste, poor planning, or just plain ignorance of outer-coast weather that shaped what happened next? In late 1906, materials were shipped to Bamfield and a road cut through the forest directly to the site. As usual, it rained. Then it rained some more. That much everyone understood.

Respected contractor George Frost had even studied the local topography. The site would be at the top of a sheer cliff, thirty-six metres above the surf. True, the cliff was undercut by ledges, but trees and their long thin roots seemed to hold everything in place. There was no sign of rockfall. Rain delayed construction, but by January 1907 the pyramidal wooden tower standing tall at the cliff edge was almost done. Then it rained in earnest. In February 1907, a landslide carried away the lot, and they had to start again—in a place that, at the time, didn't really have a name.

THE NAME Before 1905, any ship inbound from the Orient or San Francisco that missed the entrance to the Strait of Juan de Fuca was doomed. The critical thing was the correct timing of the turn eastwards from the open Pacific into the strait. A miscalculation of one's dead-reckoning position; an ignorance of the sweeping northwesterly current, the southeast gales, a lee shore; or the lack of visual references would have had any vessel booming blithely through the fog or stygian darkness, running headlong into a wall of rock.

It happened before the *Valencia* tragedy, and it would happen again, giving the outer coast between Port Renfrew and Barkley Sound the dubious and alarming epithet Graveyard of the Pacific. On July 27, 1879, under full sail, the barque *Becherdass-Ambiadass* stormed onto the rocks below the point. Although no one was lost, the point was named for a time Beghadoss Point, after the ship's Parsee name. The same thing happened in much the same place with the loss of the *Sarah* in November 1891, the *Janet Cowen* in December 1895, the *Soquel* in January 1909, the *Varsity* in February 1940, and the *Uzbekistan* in April 1943. The place was soon littered with bodies and wrecks.[98]

The Pacheedaht Nation is related both to the Makah of the Olympic Peninsula and the Ditidaht, who lived north of Port San Juan. Although they are not aligned politically, the Pacheedaht are a subgroup of the Nuu-chah-nulth. They speak a form of the Southern Wakashan and have inhabited the southern outer coast for thousands of years. Some say that the name Pachena is derived from the Ditidaht name of a village at Port Renfrew. Others believe that Indigenous hunters along the coast used the word *pacheenah*, "seafoam," when speaking of the surf beneath Beghadoss Point. The place became known as Pachena Point, which was easier for white Canadians to pronounce.[99]

DESIGN AND CONSTRUCTION Chagrined and a little stressed by the landslide, contractor George Frost chose a new site a little

▲ *Steller sea lions with the alpha male in the centre of his harem.*

farther back from the cliff and implored his men to press on and make up for lost time and effort. They did, and by August 1907, the lighthouse was complete. Frost had built a cedar-shingled ten-metre pyramidal tower with a large enough dwelling for the keeper and his assistant. Another outbuilding housed the compressed-air foghorn with its diesel engines. Federal lighthouse agent James Gaudin made sure the keepers had a code book, a set of marine alphabetic code flags, and a mast from which to fly them in order to communicate with passing ships. The temporary vapour lantern would have to do until a special one arrived from Britain. The old trail beneath the telegraph line from Carmanah Point to Bamfield was widened into a life-saving trail for shipwrecked survivors. Shelters containing blankets, dry goods, a telegraph, and instructions for its use in several languages were placed along it every few kilometres. Linesmen patrolling the line were told to carry a Lyle gun, enabling a lifeline to be shot farther across the surf than a man's throw, to a vessel in peril on the inshore rocks.

There was already a light at Carmanah Point farther south down the coast, but the Carmanah Lighthouse was not as high as it ought to have been, nor was its light (a seventh-order lamp) very bright. Pachena Point would be different. It would have the brightest and best light available. The lens system alone (two bulls-eye lenses) would be three metres high and 6.5 metres wide. Its hundreds of glass prisms would be mounted in a bronze frame and, when combined with a metal pan capable of holding 450 kilograms of small balls of liquid mercury and a clockwork apparatus for rotating the whole structure, it would weigh in at some twenty tons. It finally arrived at Pachena Point from Chance Brothers in Birmingham via Cape Horn in February 1908. When it was lit by Pachena's first keeper, John Richardson, on the evening of May 21, 1908, light keepers at the Tatoosh Lighthouse across the Strait of Juan de Fuca, some *fifty-six kilometres away,* were astonished to clearly see its double flash.[100]

THE KEEPERS John Richardson remained at Pachena Point just over a year. He was single and had brought with him his sister, Gertrude, to act as assistant keeper. The isolation proved too much for her, and she soon became severely depressed. In November 1908, she jumped to her death from the cliff in front of the tower. John left the station soon after.

The distance from Port Renfrew to Bamfield, the length of the Dominion Lifesaving Trail (now the West Coast Trail), is seventy-five kilometres. Initially, lighthouses were placed only at Carmanah and Cape Beale, but after the *Valencia* tragedy, Pachena Lighthouse closed that gap. Because of it position, Pachena also became a live-in station for telegraph linesmen and their families. Huts were built for them and the ground floor of the tower became a makeshift schoolroom.

By the 1920s the light station boasted a new wireless hut, and by the late 1930s confused telegraphers were being introduced to the wonders of radio-direction apparatus. Then World War II happened. The bombardment of the Estevan Point Lighthouse on June 20, 1942, certainly gave light keepers farther south something to think about, especially after the station's light tower

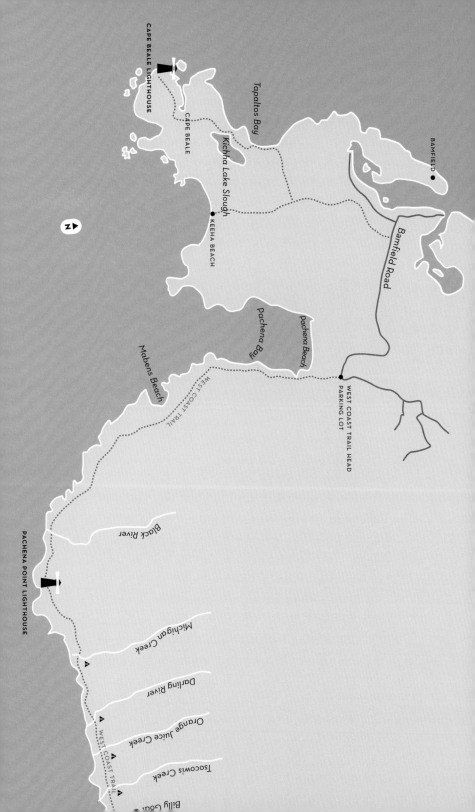

and outbuildings were painted a camouflage grey and its penetrating, life-saving lamp was extinguished.

In April 1943, Richard Wells was fifteen and had just begun his first summer job at the light station. Just after 11:00 p.m. on April 20, he and others heard what seemed to be the sound of heavy guns nearby. Minutes later, they saw a light storm of rocket flares illuminating the night sky. Were the flares to aid the aiming of the guns? Was this a full-fledged Axis attack? Richard ran towards the conflagration. In the blackout, the Russian freighter SS *Uzbekistan,* working as an American Liberty ship and inbound for Seattle, did what so many other ships did in the darkness years before. It missed the turn into the Strait of Juan de Fuca and came crashing ashore in a gale at Tsocowis Creek, just south of Pachena Point. The gunfire and rockets were from the ship trying to attract attention to its plight.

Once the position of the *Uzbekistan* was established, radio operators at Pachena Point alerted the navy and the Canadian Militia. Ships and soldiers converged. At the wreck site the next afternoon, the crew scrambled ashore at low tide, carrying as many supplies as they could manage. They caught a runaway pig on the beach, and with a roaring bonfire had a merry old time until rescuers led them along the thirty-two-kilometre trail to Bamfield.

A week later, the *Uzbekistan* captain returned to his ship only to find it buckled, keel-broken, and vandalized. This being wartime, little news of the incident was allowed to be published, though it was reported by some that the light at Pachena Point was illuminated again the next week.

In 1950, the radio shack at Pachena Point was moved north, nearer Bamfield. In the 1970s, the whole area became a national park, and the life-saving trail became the West Coast Trail. In 1997, the massive Fresnel-lens lamp was replaced with an electric pole lamp nearer the cliff edge. The lighthouse was declared a National Historic Site soon after. The station is still manned today.

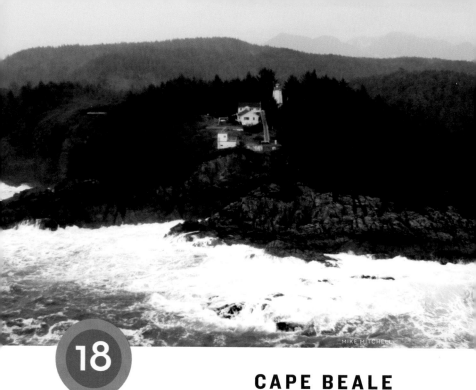

MIKE MITCHELL

18 CAPE BEALE

LAT 48°47′11″ N, **LONG** 125°12′56″ W

ACCESSIBILITY ❹ Hard

GETTING THERE The only reason the trail to Cape Beale Lighthouse is not rated "Really, Really Hard" is that it does not require an open-ocean crossing. But it is a wet, long slog through swampy bottomland on a hidden trail, replete with deadfall, overgrown trees, muddy scrambles, and a race across a watery tombolo.

On paper, the Keeha Beach–Cape Beale trail looks easy, as the route is only about six kilometres each way, but it's been called the muddiest trail on Vancouver Island. Yet, for intrepid, experienced hikers looking for a two-day, non-touristy challenge, the trek to the lighthouse is something you'll relish having done for years to come. First is an eighty-kilometre drive to Bamfield from Port Alberni. The trailhead is located at the end of Imperial Eagle Road, where there's a small parking area.

About three kilometres from the trailhead is a fork. Take the left-hand route to Keeha Beach—a good spot to camp overnight. The tidal pools are mesmerizing, so don't forget to camp above the high-tide line. Backtrack to the fork and proceed on the right-hand route to Tapaltos Bay/Cape Beale. From here the trail gets really rough and is at times obscured. You'll need flag tape and sharp eyes. The Kichha Lake slough is about three kilometres farther, but it will take two or three hours to do this stretch as it passes through a swampy bog, then rises over a slippery, steep hillock to Tapaltos Bay. The lighthouse is another two kilometres down the beach. At Cape Beale, you'll need to cross a tombolo to the islet, so be sure to check the tide tables, and only make the crossing at low tide. (At high tide, the crossing is covered with two metres of swirling ocean.) If you make it, say hello to the keeper, and check your watch or you'll be stranded for another six hours. Hope for sunny weather. What an adventure!

THE WEIRD An early, somewhat naive light keeper decided to take along a cow to his isolated posting on the west coast of Vancouver Island at Cape Beale, the very outer tip of Barkley Sound. The idea was a good one, as fresh milk would be scarce. But the plan was a dud. The cow soon became completely unhinged with loneliness. However, when fog threatened to obscure the light, a nearby wave-activated buoy on the ocean regularly brayed out its moaning, mooing message. The lonely animal was moonstruck and became besotted with the strangely familiar, lowing bawl. Even the Victoria *Daily Colonist* reported on the spectacle: "Back and forth across the water, all night and for the next few days, went the friendly exchanges between the buoy and the cow."[101]

THE NAME The Hesquiaht and Ohiaht peoples lived on the outer coast of Vancouver Island for centuries before first contact. Yet survival, even on the lush coast, meant continually being on the move. In summer, the intertidal zone and woods flourished. In the fall, salmon returning from the sea were everywhere. When the rains came, the people moved inland to winter camps and hunted deer and other game away from the deluge. Inevitably, the two groups merged into the Tla-o-qui-aht First Nation. In 1790, the Spanish explorer Francisco de Eliza was sent from Mexico to reoccupy the coast's Spanish territory, and for a time he did, naming the place Punta de Algeria. Yet, British trader Charles Barkley had already named it Cape Beale in 1787, after John Beale, his purser on the *Imperial Eagle*. Beale, along with six others, had been killed by local First Nations. But in 1794, the Nootka Convention axed the Spanish name and restored its British one.[102]

DESIGN AND CONSTRUCTION Prior to 1874, there were no navigational aids whatsoever along the west coast of Vancouver Island. It was unsettled wilderness save for Aboriginal villages; it consisted of hundreds of kilometres of first-growth timber, and the fossilized bones of prehistoric animals, which were later unearthed through construction works. The Cape Beale Lighthouse was to be the first light station on the outer coast. It was built in anticipation of increased shipping through Barkley Sound forged in the belief that nearby Port Alberni, down Alberni Inlet, would become the major export terminus for rail goods from across Canada once the Canadian Pacific Railway was completed. That never happened.

Years early of the railway achievement, a substantial lighthouse was begun in 1874, but its construction was not easy. The site, atop a craggy bluff on a tombolo at Cape Beale, was dangerously steep and inaccessible to labourers from the sea because of the tides and horrific breakers. In consequence, Huu-ay-aht people from the nearby village of Dodger Cove were hired to raft the lumber through the surf and then carry it load by load, up the escarpment. The actual builders, Haywood and Jenkinson of Victoria, along with the Indigenous workers, hiked in loadless along a safer eight-kilometre trail from Bamfield.

The original tapered wooden tower, boasting a height of eleven metres, proved worthy of its builders and lasted eight-four years. It was fitted with a lamp gallery containing a heavy, bright, second-order Fresnel wick lamp, which rotated on a base of mercury to reduce friction.[103] The combined height above the water of the bluff and tower was over forty-eight metres and warned mariners thirty kilometres out at sea of the dangerous inshore reefs at the entrance to Barkley Sound. In 1908, a louder, more strident, compressed-air diaphone replaced the lowing lament of the original foghorn. In 1958, the tower was replaced with an open, steel-framed structure, which is quite rare on this coast. Its exposed twisting staircase up through the middle of the tower to the light gallery often caught its wearied keepers in the full force of the torrential downpours. Metal baffles, or shields, installed later around the steps, helped only marginally.[104]

THE KEEPERS   Soon after the light was lit for the first time on July 1, 1874, it didn't take long for Robert Westmoreland, Cape Beale's first keeper, to figure out that his supplies were not up to snuff. Repeated shortfalls made him suspect a lighthouse agent in Victoria was pilfering the supply funds, and he said so. That cost Westmoreland his job. In the end, the plucky keeper was vindicated when the villain was arrested. However, the agent disappeared just before coming to trial, and Westmoreland never did get his job back.

The biggest problem for the keepers of the Cape Beale Lighthouse wasn't human knavery from afar; it was the ruthless disregard for Nature. Shipwrecks were the real abomination along the Graveyard of the Pacific. Yet two outstanding rescues by Cape Beale light keepers revealed such courage that their acts reminded many on this coast of what is possible when human caring

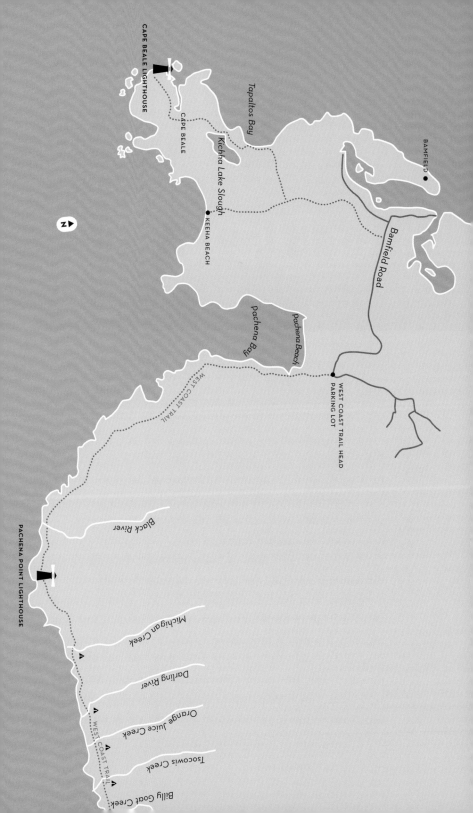

▲ *Under the rainbow beams Cape Beale Light Station.* COURTESY OF KAREN ZACHARUK

trounces indifference. Often, the light keeper's whole family became involved in averting maritime tragedy.

In August 1881, the rotating mechanism for the lamp had failed, and Cape Beale's light keeper Emmanuel Cox left with it for Victoria. In the meantime, Mrs. Cox and her three children rotated the beacon by hand, every night, all night, for fifteen days until Emmanuel returned with the repaired mechanism. The hand-rotated beacon had done its work.

In June 1890, Patti Cox, one of the light keeper's daughters, saw the full-rigged ship *Old Kensington* in danger beyond the rocks off Cape Beale. That day, her father and mother were away in Bamfield on business. Patti had seen the ship becalmed offshore and drifting inevitably, slowly towards the reefs, surf, and certain disaster. Immediately she wired Victoria for a tugboat, but the tug's agent refused to send the boat without a guarantor note of $500. Patti wired back, announcing that she would personally guarantee the demand note from her own savings. The tug arrived in the nick of time and pulled the *Old Kensington* and all who sailed in her, back out to sea. Patti Cox was just nine years old.[105]

In December 1907, loaded with lumber and unable to claw its way off a lee shore during a winter gale, the full-rigged ship *Caloma* was doomed. Heavy seas had already swept its main deck, parting the lumber, which then tore away the masts. Light keeper Tom Paterson and his wife, Minnie, watched helplessly as the seas pushed the *Caloma* towards the rocks, its crew cowering at the stern. The telephone lines were down, but Tom knew the lighthouse-supply ship *Quadra* lay stormbound in Bamfield Inlet nine kilometres away. Tom was needed for the light. What to do?

Minnie ran for it, but the tombolo separating Cape Beale from the shore was already awash with the rising tide. Minnie crossed it, waist-deep through the swirling ocean. Then breathless, she raced down the tree-strewn trail. Halfway, she reached James MacKay's cabin, but the lineman was away, so Minnie and James's wife grabbed a shoreside boat and rowed out across the inlet to the steamer. The *Quadra,* with steam up, immediately left for the stricken ship. She hove-to off the *Caloma*'s stern and sent a longboat to take off all its crew. Stopping for only a hot cup of tea with Mrs. MacKay upon their return, Minnie ran back to Cape Beale to nurse her baby. The federal government gave Minnie Paterson a medal for her bravery, but the rescue weakened her, and she died of TB five years later.

More recently, in December 1995, the fifteen-metre fishing boat *Dalewood Provider* was lost off Cape Beale in a storm in which the winds were so strong that light keeper Norbie Brand wrote in his log, "I had to crawl on [my] hands and knees to the tip of the Cape."[106] There Brand saw the overturned boat in front of the station and called the Tofino coast guard. A helicopter picked up one survivor after spotting flares in the area of Mud Bay. The two other crew members were found later, deceased. Cape Beale Lighthouse is still manned to this day.

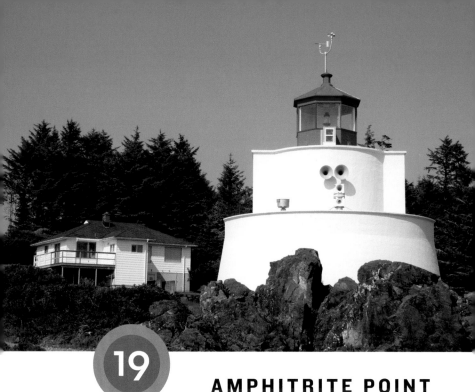

19 AMPHITRITE POINT

LAT 48°55′16″ N, **LONG** 123°32′28″ W

ACCESSIBILITY ❷ Still Easy

GETTING THERE Amphitrite Point Lighthouse is quite easy to get to, though it calls for a drive to Ucluelet on the west side of Vancouver Island. If you're visiting the coast and want a trip with unending scenic rewards, this drive is just the ticket. The paved highway (No. 4) begins about ten kilometres north of Nanaimo. It's well marked and heads west through Port Alberni to Ucluelet and Tofino. Ucluelet is much less touristy (and much cheaper) than Tofino, and you might consider staying on board the fully restored Canadian hydrographic survey vessel, the *Canadian Princess* (previously called the *William J. Stewart*), which is moored here. The *Canadian Princess* is a bit funky (no TV, and the "head" is down the hall), but it is marvellously authentic and has a great on-board restaurant and bar. Once you see the ocean, you might decide to stay an extra day and walk Long Beach at nearby Pacific Rim National Park Reserve.

There's a trail in town to the Amphitrite Point Lighthouse from the middle of town. Drive south along Peninsula Road and turn right (west), on Coast Guard Drive. The trail at the end of the road is marked.

THE WEIRD

FROM THE *DAILY COLONIST*: *Without benefit of clergy, with no priest or minister present to read the last rites over the bruised bodies, the remains of the seamen of the wrecked, steel barque,* Pass of Melfort, *whose bodies were recovered from the sea, were laid away in the little village graveyard at Ucluelet while the assembled knelt and offered a prayer for the dead.*

In Memory of the Lost.

Harry Scougall, Capt.; W. Baldwin, Hans Meyer,
L.B. Brown, George Planders, Charles Hayes, E. Crawford,
J. Liva, L. Bruce, J. Kern, J.H. Jopling, E. Weijonen, F. Swenson,
G. Abraham, John Kirchman, D. McInnes, W. Wormell,
G. Hardwick, G. Phillips, R. Sharpie, John Seaton, D. G. Retrie,
A. Grant, F.G.G. Richer, A. Kipling, Dan Rosette,
Thom Kelly, and one unidentified woman.[107]

The *Pass of Melfort* was a big ship, a barque of 2,346 gross tons, over ninety-one metres long. It was built in Scotland in 1890 and one of the last "moonrakers" of her time. Its three high masts were square-rigged; its fourth, the mizzen, was rigged fore and aft, and, like its sister ships, it could really move, making Cardiff, Wales, from Lima, Peru, in fifty-eight days. The *Pass of Melfort* was last seen by Captain Olsen on the *Brodick Castle* off southern California. Flag-semaphore communication established she was twenty-three days out from Panama, bound for lumber in Puget Sound. Captain Olsen expected the ship would arrive before him, but secretly he feared the worst.[108]

▲ *It is thought that the squat reinforced-concrete tower could survive any tsunami.*

The worst happened on December 23, 1905. A horrific south-east storm drove the *Pass of Melfort* onto a reef on the lee shore of Vancouver Island forty-five metres from Amphitrite Point. An old salt, Captain Olsen reported that he nearly lost his *Brodick Castle* in that same storm. "It was the toughest bit of sailing I've ever done," he said. Local First Nations told of rockets being fired from the doomed ship at dawn, and villagers from Ucluelet found splintered wreckage in a rock-strewn bay at the point. Everyone on board perished.

Men stood in the still-boiling surf all day with long boat-hooks retrieving bodies as they rolled back and forth in the waves. One still bled from gashes to the skull. Another was that of a teenager, presumably an apprentice. A woman, still wearing a new grey-cloth coat with red trim, was presumed to be the captain's wife.

Like the wreck of the *Valencia*, it took the tragedy of the *Pass of Melfort* to get a proper lighthouse at Amphitrite Point, and even then it didn't come easily and it took many years.

THE NAME Ucluelet means "people of the safe harbour" in the Nuu-chah-nulth language. The village of Ucluelet stands at the southern end of a long peninsula bordering the northwest side of Barkley Sound on the west coast of Vancouver Island. For generations, First Nations set out from Hitacu, a village opposite Ucluelet, venturing far out into the open Pacific to hunt migrating whales from their revered and seaworthy canoes.

The British renamed the place Amphitrite Point after HMS *Amphitrite*, a three-masted Royal Navy gunboat that was stationed in Esquimalt from 1851 to 1857. In Greek mythology, Amphitrite was the wife of Poseidon and goddess of the sea. The Greeks clearly understood human frailty and the supremacy of Fate.

DESIGN AND CONSTRUCTION   It was believed that the whistling buoy marking the reef in Carolina Channel had been ripped from its chains during the storm, so sailors naturally demanded a proper, shoreside light station. In response, the federal government spent a measly $140 to build a small square tower at the point housing a three-wick, thirty-one-day Wigham oil lamp. James Fraser, a coxswain from the coast guard station at Ucluelet, had the extra job of attending the lamp daily. That original tower lasted only until January 2, 1914, when a tsunami smashed it to pieces. Hastily the government built another cheap square

▼ **left** *Amphitrite's first concrete tower (1916), and its predessesor, a temporary lookout tower* **(right)** *built after the original lighthouse was washed away in a tsunami on January 2, 1914.* CITY OF VANCOUVER ARCHIVES

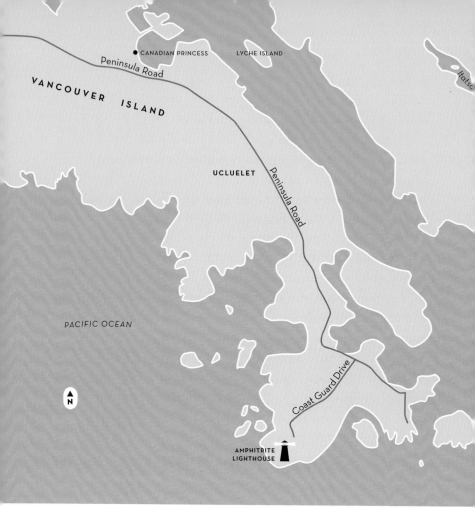

wooden spotting tower a little farther back from the point, and it hung a smaller replacement lamp inside.

THE KEEPERS The public demanded more, and finally in January 1915, construction began on a six-metre-high squat, round concrete lighthouse, with a flashing (rotating) white light and foghorn. The whole stubby structure was firmly attached to a blasted-flat rock base at the point. Yet, even then, the tower had no dwelling for a keeper, and for three years the coast guard had to manage the light. By 1918, the coast guard was fed up with the

Anomalies and Ironies

1 There was a scrap of paper taken from the surf the day the *Pass of Melfort* came ashore, bearing the name of John Houston. His remains were never found. It was later determined that the paper was from the *Melfort*'s log and Houston was a former captain. He had booked off just before the ship's last fateful voyage.

2 Other telling bits of debris were recovered from the wreckage. One was the carved effigy of a young woman; it was the ship's wooden figurehead from beneath the *Melfort*'s bowsprit, glistening innocent and white in the surf. It was claimed that it was both a foreshadowing and a lament for the missing captain's wife, Mrs. Scougall, whose body they found later.

3 In 1987, in spite of protests, the Canadian Coast Guard set about de-staffing west coast lighthouses. They paused briefly to consider the government's decision, then in 1988 went ahead and de-staffed five lighthouses on the west coast. Amphitrite Point Lighthouse was one of those that lost its keeper. So much for the lesson inherent in the loss of the *Pass of Melfort*.

extra work and the government took on the coxswain and made him Amphitrite's keeper.

But James Fraser couldn't live at the station, as there was no accommodation. So he was required to walk from town, each day—at dusk to light the lamp and again at midnight to rewind the rotating mechanism, walk home, and return twice again before the morning's hike out at dawn to extinguish the wick. He did this for 365 days, sleet, hurricanes, and torrential rains be damned. For his trouble, he was paid $10 a month. He quit a year later, in 1919.

His replacement, Fred Routcliffe, squeezed a bed into the tower beside the noisy diaphone apparatus and resigned himself to such an existence for ten years. He complained finally, stoically, arguing that it was just the leaks and the damp during the rains that made the place unfit.[109] Eventually, in 1929, the Department of Marine built a keeper's house well behind the tower and, wonder of wonders, even equipped the place with a telephone.

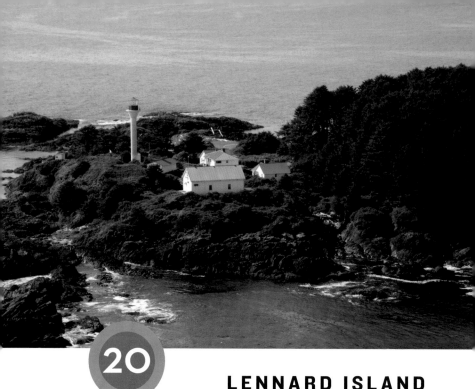

20

LENNARD ISLAND

LAT 49°06′40″ N, **LONG** 125°55′21″ W

ACCESSIBILITY ❺ Really, Really Hard

GETTING THERE   Though only five kilometres from Tofino on the west coast of Vancouver Island, the lighthouse lies on the seawards side of Lennard Island and thereby receives the full impact of the five thousand–kilometre open fetch of the Pacific Ocean. At the best of times, fierce swells make landings extremely difficult. At most other times, when there are storms, any kind of landing is considered completely impossible.

Getting out to Lennard Island for a visit is just about impossible. If you can finagle a ride with the coast guard or a qualified tourist-adventure company in Tofino, terrific—but don't go alone, especially by kayak or in a small boat. The sea is never flat. In calm weather, three-metre-high ocean swells from Japan surge regularly upon the rocks below the station. Yet even if you only see the lighthouse on Lennard Island from Cox Bay or Chesterman Beach near Tofino, the drive across Vancouver Island to see that part of this magical coast is, for many explorers, reward enough.

THE WEIRD When Charles Barrett-Lennard stepped ashore from his yacht *Templar* at Nootka in 1860, he witnessed a local chief act out a strange welcoming ceremony. What Barrett-Lennard didn't know was the origin of the ceremony. In 1788, a Mowachaht chief had injured himself while climbing up on board John Meares's small ship *Felice*. The *Felice*'s surgeon stitched up the injured chief, shook his hand, and sent him away. Now, seventy years later, the chief standing before Barrett-Lennard pantomimed that same medical encounter as a ceremonial greeting. The astonished Barrett-Lennard believed that the formal salutation was a symbolic re-enactment of James Cook's landing.[110]

THE NAME Lennard Island is named after the gentleman-adventurer whose lineage went back as far as King James I. In Middle English, Barrett was typically a first name meaning "lively and strong." It became a surname in the eighteenth century. The spirited Charles Edward Barrett-Lennard was born in 1835, the grandson of Sir Thomas Barrett-Lennard, 1st Baronet of Belhus, Essex, and like many sons of the aristocracy at the time, he chose the army as a future befitting a nobleman of his station.

As a young man, Barrett-Lennard joined the 5th Dragoon Guards, but soon tired of the cocktails and mannered constraints of a young officer's life, so in 1860 he put his small yacht, *Templar*, on the deck of the ship *Athelstan* and arrived in Victoria in March 1860. On board he befriended another ex-military officer, Fitz Stubbs, and together they made the first complete circumnavigation of Vancouver Island. At the time, there were no navigational aids and few charts for such a wild adventure. So, Barrett-Lennard's voyage in a fifteen-metre sailing cutter was considered quite remarkable. In 1861, Captain Richards of the survey ship HMS *Hecate* credited Barrett-Lennard's feat by naming a small islet off Tofino in his honour: Lennard Island.[111]

DESIGN AND CONSTRUCTION   Barely a few hundred metres long, the small teardrop-shaped Lennard Island is only just visible from Tofino. Located at the southwestern end of Templar Channel, it marks the entrance of a passage leading to the calmer waters off Tofino and Clayoquot Sound. Settlements followed the resource-rich endowments of Barkley and Nootka Sounds, and Clayoquot Sound was no exception. Another lighthouse was needed here, some eighty kilometres north of Cape Beale, not just for the sealers, or for the supply and mail ships serving this part of the perilous coast. It was needed as a landfall (and as a second bearing) for the smart CPR liners inbound from Asia. Marine interests lobbied furiously. Ottawa took notice.

In 1903, enough trees were cleared away to build a dwelling and a lighthouse on the southwestern tip of the island, and the next year George Frost supervised materials and sent up a crew

▼ **left** *Lennard's first-order lamp.* **right** *Coast guard Santa George E. Thomas with two sets of keepers' children: Davis and Bill McNeil and Sharon and Elanie Bruton, circa 1967.* COURTESY OF S. BRUTON

of workmen on the steamer *Quadra*. The lighthouse would be a sturdy wooden octagonal tower some ten metres high. The clearing upon which it stood raised the combined elevation to over thirty metres above high water. But the tower's most distinctive feature was the lamp. No costs were spared to obtain the largest Fresnel-lens light ever made for this treacherous, fog-enshrouded coast. The twenty-ton, first-order dioptric Chance Brothers lamp had a lens that was over two metres tall. Its petroleum-fed burner, which vaporized on an incandescent mantle, sent a beam some twenty-five kilometres out into the darkness. The clockwork rotation apparatus alone contained over 360 kilograms of miniscule balls of liquid mercury, enough to float the massive lamp-housing and have it move at the touch of a finger.[112] Years later, when electricity replaced the clockwork mechanism, it was said the structure was so well balanced, it only required the operation of a quarter-horsepower motor.

A year later, a steam-driven diaphone was added to the station in its own building and, optimistically, a boat landing was blasted out from a cleft in the nearby shoreside rocks.

THE KEEPERS Frank Garrard, Lennard Island's first keeper, had sailed the seven seas, prospected, farmed, and even worked for George Frost during the construction of Cape Beale Lighthouse. In short, he was the perfect man for the job. The trouble was he brought along his wife, Annie, and his six school-age children. Annie was hired as an assistant keeper to manage the foghorn and assist in the winding of the rotation apparatus, which had to be wound every three hours, twenty-four hours per day. She also had to feed the family, keep house, and take care of the hens, cows, and kids. But first, they all had to witness a mighty tempest.

On December 23, 1905, one of the fiercest winter storms to ever hit the west coast, pummelled Barkley and Clayoquot Sounds. In nearby Barkley Sound the huge barque *Pass of Melfort* was driven onto the rocks at Amphitrite Point by hurricane-force winds. Everyone on board perished. It would be a portent of things to come for the Garrard family and their children.

Lilly, the oldest daughter, was safe from such horrors because she worked as an au pair in Tofino and went to high school in Victoria during the week. The others were not so lucky. Although Ethel, Noel, and Olive boarded in Tofino during the week and went to elementary school, they were expected home on weekends. For the trip, Father provided them with a large, lapstrake, double-ended rowing canoe. Frank would row halfway down Templar Channel to meet the kids in the larger station boat on Friday afternoons and shepherd them, convoy fashion, to their warm if soon messy digs for two days of glorious freedom from school.

One Friday, the canoe capsized when an oarlock broke and the children stood up in the small craft to rig a sail. Their father and others watched what happened from the approaching station's longboat. Noel was able to climb up onto the overturned hull, while Ethel, gasping nearby, held on to her sister, Olive, who was thrashing frantically in the water. The North Pacific is very cold, and once hypothermia sets in, a small child can die in minutes. Father saved them all, but only just. Once they were safely ashore on Lennard Island, he sawed the rowing canoe in half and made two troughs to feed the cows. Nightmares loomed.

In November 1906, Annie had her seventh child, Edward. In the spring, lighthouse inspector Gordon Halkett had them scrambling to clean the station, top to bottom. They had already received one bad report; another could cost Garrard his job. Unguarded for a moment in the scrubbing melee, baby Edward ingested some lye, a cleaning agent. He died a few days later. The Garrards left Lennard Island the following year.[113]

In 1932, a series of winter storms prevented keeper Thomas McNab from getting into town for the mail, the Christmas gifts,

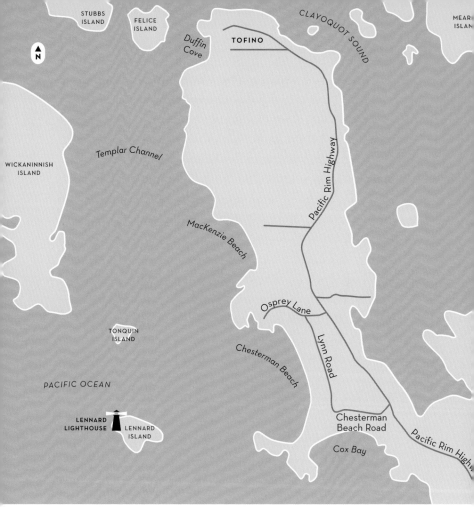

and all the fixings for his family's Christmas dinner. Fisherman Bjarne Arnet braved the tempests in his salmon troller *Pete*. In a lull, Arnet made a hair-raising dash to Lennard Island with the Yuletide supplies. The locals loved their light keepers.

But the sea took its toll on the dwellings at Lennard Island, and in 1959 two new houses were built for the keeper and his assistant. In 1970, young Sharon and Elanie Bruton heard from yard staff who where on hand that the coast guard had unceremoniously dumped pieces of the antique first-order lamp into the ocean.[114] By 1977, a diesel generator had replaced the use of oil, and collectors on the roofs of outbuildings filled a 340,000-litre tank with rainwater. The station's longboat was replaced with regular visits by the CCGS *Sir James Douglas*. When storms even made that impossible, a helipad stood ready to receive air support, though the keeper often had to remove sea-blown logs from its top some twenty-one metres above the water.

By 1977, Stephen Holland, the keeper's ten-year-old son, his younger brother, David, and their parents were regularly receiving a special three-month allotment of sixty-five books from the Victoria public library. That, along with the boys' correspondence-school coursework, perhaps made the boys glum, but it all faded when *Sir James Douglas* showed up with buckets of ice cream, fresh fruit and vegetables, tools, and 170-litre drums of gasoline—all of which had to be basketed and winched up to the station by an overhead cable trolley. Official advance-poll ballots enabling their parents to vote most always arrived by helicopter. In Tofino, a swift coast-guard lifeboat stood by, ever ready.[115]

By the 1980s, life at Lennard Island had been transformed. The Holland boys stood with their feet in two vastly different worlds. They could identify sea anemones in tidal pools mere metres from home and build log forts on the foreshore. They could handle a boat, build log forts, and examine all sorts of marine life in the ubiquitous small tidal pools. They could operate the foghorn, maintain the light, manhandle a winch, and use a radio-telephone as naturally as urban children rode bicycles. At the same time, they were beginning to use computers, do chemistry experiments as dictated by their distance-education teachers, and solve math problems with a hefty dose of pragmatic intelligence, all of which was nurtured through lives having direct contact with the sea.

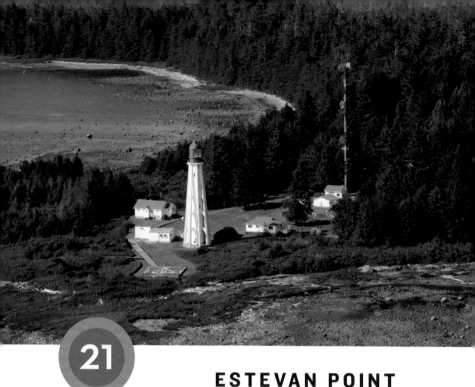

21 ESTEVAN POINT

LAT 49°38′29″ N, **LONG** 126°54′40″ W

ACCESSIBILITY ⑤ Really, Really Hard

GETTING THERE Midway up the west coast of Vancouver Island, Estevan Point Lighthouse sees few outsiders. Reachable through Hesquiat Peninsula Provincial Park, it is a trip only for experienced hikers with lots of time and real intent. However, if you do go, it's an adventure of a lifetime.

I was lucky enough to land at Estevan Lighthouse having been transported there by helicopter pilot Glenn Daichuk in 1998 while researching another book (*Glyphs and Gallows*) about Hesquiaht history. I don't think I would have made it to the site any other way. Flying close to the water and coming up to the white, glistening tower over the flat and foaming foreshore was absolutely magnificent.

Hesquiat Peninsula is now a provincial park, but there are no clearly designated trails. The old trail from the lighthouse

▲ *Note the modern radio/microwave/GPS tower to the left of the station buildings.*

through to the village of Hesquiat was, when I was there last, already heavily grown over. One way to see Estevan Lighthouse is to charter a boat from Tahsis or Gold River. Tahtsa Dive Charters offers two vessels that service Nootka Sound. Maxi's Water Taxi has a twelve-passenger, coast guard–approved vessel. Drive to Campbell River, then take Highway 28 to Gold River. Turn left at the information centre in town and drive fourteen kilometres to the government wharf. Be sure to make arrangements before you go.

If you are a true lighthouse aficionado and can afford it, Air Nootka from Gold River or Tofino Air from Tofino will land you, weather permitting, at Escalante Point some fifty kilometres from the site; you can hike in and around the peninsula and be picked up in Boat Basin. It is a wild place, and bears, eagles, cormorants, and seals abound, so go in with an experienced group and be fully prepared to hunker down for days on end during inclement weather. Post a plan and take your time. This magnificent adventure will not only give you bragging rights, but it will also leave you with a grin as large as the keeper's children of another time.

THE WEIRD Was it a genuine wartime attack or a government ruse? Some historians still argue about this. On June 20, 1942, Estevan Point light keeper Robert Lally and radio operator Edward Redford reported their lighthouse being bombed by twenty shells from a warship some five kilometres offshore. Along with the cruiser they reported another smaller vessel and a submarine. Lally's son and his friend Mina Chamberlain (both nine years old at the time) confirmed the sightings. It was known that two Japanese submarines (J-26 and I-26) had previously been spotted off the Oregon coast, and Canadian warships had been on patrol off northern Vancouver Island just days before. The warships' sweep of the area found nothing. The Fisheries and Naval reserve vessel HMCS *Mooloch* was dispatched to Estevan Point. There, the Royal Canadian Navy seized a 140 mm shell casing with familiar Japanese yellow markings. Yet some reports also claimed that the casing had vaguely recognizable English lettering on its underside.

Later, a theory emerged that Robert Lally's original story was altered by members of the war cabinet to report only the submarine attack. Strangely, the shell casing and parts of Lally's Estevan logbook, which recorded the sighting and was seized, went missing. Mina Peet (née Chamberlain) later concurred with earlier reports that the navy visited the lighthouse soon after the bombing and removed certain pages from that book. Officially, Ottawa bureaucrats claimed that Robert Lally was "under stress" when he reported the attack, perhaps implying that his testimony may have been unreliable due to his state of mind. Although his assistant and two children denied this claim, the public came to believe that Lally and the others didn't see anything like a battleship that day.

Adding to the intrigue was the fact that Prime Minister Mackenzie King was in a parliamentary deadlock over the conscription issue, and his diary curiously reveals his elation over the Estevan Point barrage. There is even evidence to suggest it was Canadian or American warships that were ordered to fire upon Estevan Point Lighthouse in order to galvanize public opinion in favour of backing the conscription debate.[116] To the end, Robert Lally swore it was a battle cruiser he saw and not a submarine that fired upon Estevan Lighthouse.

THE NAME The enormously wide Hesquiat Peninsula forms the southern boundary of Nootka Sound, and for hundreds of years it was the ancestral home of five distinct Nuu-chah-nulth settlements. In the early 1800s, they amalgamated into one village, at Hesquiat. Estevan Point lies at the westernmost tip of the peninsula. The name Hesquiat is an English derivative of *Heish-kwi-aht* or *Heish-heish-a*, meaning "to tear asunder with the teeth." It referred to the Indigenous practice of using their teeth to strip herring spawn off the saltwater eelgrass, which grew inshore at Hesquiat. The spawn was considered a delicacy.[117]

Estevan Point was named by Spanish commander Juan Perez in 1774, after his second lieutenant Esteban José Martínez. In 1789, trained as a naval officer and navigator in Seville, Martínez was ordered by the viceroy of New Spain (Mexico) to occupy Nootka Sound. There, he built a settlement (Santa Cruz de Nuca) and a fort (Fort San Miguel). However, British and Russian threats against Spanish sovereignty caused him that summer to seize several British ships and arrest their crews, precipitating the Nootka Crisis. Esteban Martínez was instrumental in the Spanish exploration of Canada's outer west coast.

DESIGN AND CONSTRUCTION Estevan Point faces the full wrath of the open Pacific Ocean, and there is absolutely no chance of a permanent wharf anywhere near the site that could survive the continuous onslaught of the seas. So, throughout the summer of 1907, the steamer *Maude* was forced to unload sixty thousand board feet of lumber in a bay some 3.5 kilometres west of Estevan Point. There, labourers began the construction of a tramway to carry all the materials back around to the rocky, remote tip of the Hesquiat Peninsula.

Initially, the local Hesquiaht people were friendly towards the lighthouse builders, but they gradually grew resentful as they saw their ancestral homeland being defiled during the construction. In May 1908, a group from the Hesquiaht band raided the site and destroyed several buildings under construction. Builders, suppliers, keepers, and their families felt uneasy for many years following that episode.[118]

Throughout the summers of 1908 and 1909, the concrete forms slowly gave shape to an octagonal free-standing tower capable of holding an extra nine-metre-high, twenty-five-ton light assembly in a lamp gallery some thirty-one metres above the ground. The trick to Estevan Point's strength and durability lay in the use of Colonel William P. Anderson's famed flying buttresses. Anderson was an engineer and head of the Canadian Lighthouse Board and had developed the detached, triple-braced supports early in his career. Six of the slender, slightly arched abutments not only provided a durable exoskeleton for the tower, but they also created a structure of great architectural beauty. When it was completed in 1910, the Estevan Point Lighthouse ranked among Anderson's finest achievements and was easily one of his most elegant designs.

One worker, having spent many months far from the ground, proclaimed, "Even in the most severe gales, the tower scarcely vibrated."[119] Anderson's design proved worthy because on December 6, 1918, Estevan Point Lighthouse was rocked by a strong earthquake. Small pieces of the concrete were ejected from the structure leaving some pronounced cracks, but the tower stood firm. The major damage was to the $35,000 first-order

Chance Brothers Fresnel-lens light assembly, which sat forty metres above the ground, high in the lamp room. The brightest light on the west coast had sustained damage to some of its prisms and mirrors, and many of the mercury balls used to support its twenty-five-ton weight and enabling its easy rotation had spilled. But beyond that, all was well. That day, the light keeper reported that he felt ten distinctly powerful shocks. A lesser tower would have collapsed completely.[120]

THE KEEPERS   Otto Buckholtz was hired from among the work crew to become Estevan Point Lighthouse's first keeper. He also had previous experience as a sealer and knew the ways of the ocean. What he didn't have, presumably, were interpersonal skills because within a year he had become embroiled in a conflict with local Hesquiaht people, which culminated in Buckholtz shooting a cow. The Hesquiaht demanded that he be arrested; cows were a precious commodity on this desolate coast. According to the Victoria *Daily Colonist*, "Mrs. Antoine Luckovich, wife of the storekeeper at Hesquiat, and her daughter reported that while in Victoria, her husband sent her a telegram stating the cow is shot. When the police asked for proof, she reported that he had threatened to do it."[121] A short time later, Buckholtz left the service.

Jens Jensen, Buckholtz's replacement, got on well enough with those around him, but the horrific winter storms and the frequent earthquakes unnerved him. In one letter to the federal-lighthouse agent in Victoria, he wrote that if he was not able to pass up one coming stint at Estevan, he would quit altogether.

Throughout the 1930s, life passed at Estevan Point as it did elsewhere, with the usual spats, brouhahas, and misunderstandings interrupting those confined to this most isolated outpost. In their later memories, it was the children of the keepers who reminded us of the inherent attraction and fear of Natures's overwhelming forces. Several reminisced about climbing up the tower

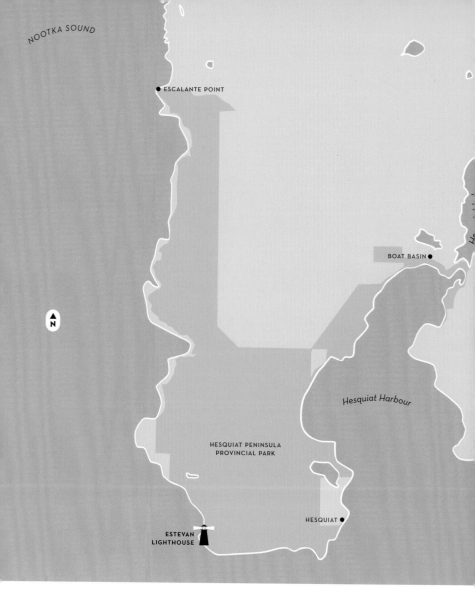

NOOTKA SOUND

ESCALANTE POINT

BOAT BASIN ●

Hesquiat Harbour

HESQUIAT PENINSULA
PROVINCIAL PARK

HESQUIAT ●

ESTEVAN
LIGHTHOUSE

to the lamp gallery and hanging onto its outside railing for dear life, as it vibrated dangerously during the full gales. With faces wet and streaming, they would yell gleefully into the void. Would they come down without parental cajoling? Not on your life.[122]

After the events of World War II, the lighthouse remained manned through the Cold War and beyond, up to the present day.

22

NOOTKA

LAT 49°35′33″ N, **LONG** 126°36′58″ W

ACCESSIBILITY ❸ Moderate

GETTING THERE   The only way to visit Nootka Lighthouse is on a magnificent day trip on board the MV *Uchuck III* from Gold River, Vancouver Island. Formerly an American minesweeper, this sturdy vessel was converted into a working coastal freighter and passenger ship and has served the waters of Nootka and Kyuquot Sounds for nearly fifty years. If you desire a remote yet doable west coast lighthouse adventure, this is it.

During the summers (Wednesdays and Saturdays) the MV *Uchuck III* runs from Gold River to Friendly Cove (Yuquot, on Nootka Island). Along the way it services such isolated logging camps as McCurdy Creek, Houston River, and Mooyah Bay. All are situated along Muchalat Inlet as it winds its way down to the sound and to the sea. You'll see black bears, bald eagles, dolphins, whales, and sometimes even sea otters. You'll also pass close by Resolution Cove on Bligh Island (named after the Captain Bligh of the HMS *Bounty*). It's where James Cook careened HMS *Resolution* over on its side to clean its bottom of barnacles and sea slime. You can actually see the circle of stones along the beach where *Resolution*'s crew removed them from the shallow water before hauling the vessel onto its side! And that's before you reach Yuquot! On board, you'll meet kayakers being dropped off in Nootka Sound and intrepid hikers heading for the thirty-seven-kilometre Nootka Trail. It's all very relaxed, with a lounge and canteen on board (they serve great chili). There's plenty of outside seating where the raw west coast presents itself at its unparalleled best. Reserve a spot on board early.

At Yuquot, there is just enough time to see the ruins of Fort San Miguel and the settlement of Santa Cruz de Nuca, established by Esteban José Martínez in 1789. Visit the lighthouse grounds, and walk the shingle beach at Friendly Cove. The old Catholic church and its stained-glass window is testament to an earlier side of Mowachaht/Muchalaht culture, as are the remains of several large totem poles. On other days, the *Uchuck III* goes farther north to Kyuquot Sound. It's an overnight trip, with accommodations at Kyuquot included in the price of the ticket. I've done both trips several times, and each time the place reverberates with its amazing history.

Drive north from Nanaimo on Highway 19, then turn west on Highway 28 to Gold River. Follow the signs. You'll need to stay in Gold River overnight, because the ship leaves promptly at 7:00 a.m. from its wharf, some eight kilometres west of town. Be on time!

To be a genuine Canadian, you must stand on the same far western shore that James Cook stood upon over two hundred years ago, just as you must stand upon the citadel of Old Quebec and beside the Cabot Tower on Signal Hill in St. John's, Newfoundland and Labrador. Don't argue; just go for it.

THE WEIRD By today's standards, it may not seem that weird, but the rapaciousness then was absolutely unearthly. On December 9, 1908, the Victoria *Daily Colonist* ran the following advertisement:

TIMBER IS KING ON NOOTKA SOUND.
As well as elsewhere in Canada's premier province,
choice sections, finely situated for logging
at $2.50 per acre . . .
This is a particularly good buy. Full particulars from:
Bond and Clark Co., Phone 1092
614 Trounce Avenue, P.O. Box 535 [123]

By 1830, the sea otters were gone. By 1880, the whales were seriously threatened. Then in 1884, Edgar Sayward bought 886 acres of land for $886 dollars. Nine years later, in 1893, the Sayward Mill and Timber Co. leased 7,706 acres of land in Nootka Sound for 10 cents an acre. In 1909, James Dunsmuir opened an open-pit iron mine in Tlupana Inlet.[124] Ships carrying logs and ore needed navigational guidance as they plied to and from the open Pacific. Suddenly the word was out, and workers and opportunists flocked to the place. By 1910, the Nootka land registry was doing a roaring business. Even Captain Walbran noted that "limestone, marble, iron and coal are known to exist enough in Nootka Sound to warrant the establishment of large industries."[125] Besides, just four years earlier, the steamship *Valencia* was wrecked down the coast at Pachena Point with the loss of 126 lives. Something had to be done. Industry was burgeoning in Nootka Sound, and goods and people needed protection from the cruel seas. Officials in Ottawa soon began to hear a growing clamour for a lighthouse at the mouth of this most promising northern Vancouver Island inlet.

THE NAME In 1910, Colonel William Anderson, chairman of the Department of Marine's Lighthouse Board, acted fast. He had the

▲ *Fog rolling in over Nootka Station.*

small rocky islets of San Miguel adjacent to the Aboriginal settlement of Yuquot (Friendly Cove) formally ceded to Canada.

The name Nootka, oddly, comes from Captain Cook, who was told by the Natives of the area, *"Ichme nutka,"* or "Go around" into the cove as his ship approached. Cook misunderstood, thinking that they were telling him where he was. The adverb became a noun, and Nootka became a centre for international trade and competition.

The significance of the settlement of Yuquot, meaning "wind comes from all directions," was ignored completely. For over four thousand years, the Mowachaht people had made Yuquot their summer home, protected as it was in a cove on the lee side of a small peninsula at the mouth of Nootka Sound. Here, from May to November, deer, berries, shellfish, derivative fish oils, and giant cedars were as bountiful as the returning salmon of autumn. Then, the vicious winds and rainstorms of winter forced the inhabitants farther inland to their winter camp near Tahsis at the head of Nootka Sound.

DESIGN AND CONSTRUCTION In December 1905, Captain Davidson and his crew of the disabled vessel *King David* abandoned their ship when it ran aground on Bajo Reef in the middle of Nootka Sound. Taking to the lifeboats, they reached an abandoned Aboriginal fishing camp on a far shore and presumed they were near Cape Beale, but the current had pushed their ill-fated ship farther north than they guessed. After three days, six of Davidson's men set out by lifeboat for the assumed cape which was over 160 kilometres away. The lifeboat and its crew were never seen again.

After thirty-three days at the shoreside camp, those waiting were spotted by the passing steamer *Queen City* and taken to Yuquot, only twelve kilometres away. The lifeboat must have set off in the wrong direction. A year later, in 1906, the storekeeper at Yuquot set a lamp on top of San Rafael Island, the largest of the adjacent San Miguel Islands. That story and the lamp were the impetus for the 1910 petition to Ottawa.[126]

Within a year, in February 1911, a square wooden two-storey dwelling and lean-to was built on top of a bluff on San Rafael Island at Nootka. Protruding from its roof was a balcony and light gallery that loomed thirty-three metres over the ocean. Its fixed white lamp was often lost, however, in the foggy gloom. Wages for its first keeper were set at $360 dollars per year, "less than a third of the wages paid to Native labourers" who built the station.[127]

THE KEEPERS Poor wages and poorer living conditions dogged the keepers of the Nootka Lighthouse during its first years. The wives of Herbert Smith (1911–18) and William Taylor (1918) both suffered crippling rheumatism because of the awful damp, the continually leaking roof, and the lack of a proper stove for heat. One keeper, Patrick Foley from Newfoundland, was so frustrated by Ottawa's indifference to his needs that he left after just two months.

In 1915, however, when CPR steamships complained about the lacklustre lamp, an expensive new rotating lamp housing

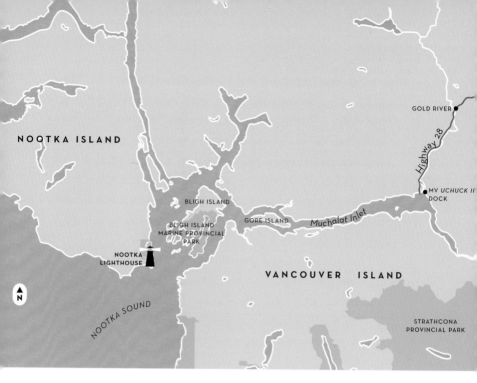

containing a brighter light gave Nootka Lighthouse its clear and distinctive white flash. That year, a foghorn was added, but to save money, the keeper had to crank it by hand. Of course, throughout the 1920s, wages remained the same.

In 1929, the annual salary for a keeper at Nootka Lighthouse rose to $1,860, but keeper Tom Fish had to pay the salary of an assistant keeper out of his own pocket. (Patrick Foley was also out of pocket for the fuel and coal for his own and his assistant's dwelling.) Although Fish was reimbursed for expenses required for the maintenance of the newly installed compressed-air diaphone and rotating lamp mechanisms, it was often late in coming. That left him as broke as his predecessors.

There were, however, bright spots. That summer of 1929, the painter Emily Carr visited Fish at Nootka Lighthouse. She described it in her diary as "a strange, wild world, perched on a nosegay of rocks, bunched with trees and spiced with wild-flowers."[128]

One couple, Ed and Pat Kidder, braved it the best. They were high school sweethearts, but were forced apart by parents who worked in different locations. When they finally arrived together at Nootka in 1970 as keepers, they generated their own heat and stayed thirteen years. Along the way they ventured out in the station's longboat to a family of six Vietnamese fishermen who failed to respond to a radio message. They found all of them unconscious from carbon-monoxide poisoning in their tightly enclosed boat.[129]

Today, the Nootka Lighthouse has been saved from destruction and is protected by Canada's Heritage Lighthouse Protection Act. Administered by Parks Canada, it will remain as one of Canada's most significant maritime symbols. As of 2014, the station was still manned.

◀ *MV Uchuck III in Nootka Sound.* COURTESY OF NEIL HAVERS DESIGN

23

PULTENEY POINT

LAT 50°37'49.9" N, **LONG** 127°09'14" W

ACCESSIBILITY ❷ Still Easy

GETTING THERE Getting to Pulteney Point is a cinch, though it requires a bit of a drive up Vancouver Island to Sointula on Malcolm Island. En route you will pass through enchanting little villages and some of the most beguiling coastal scenery in the world. It's possible to drive right to the site.

On the trip up island to Pulteney Point, you will need to pass through Port McNeill. The village is not only famous for its whale-watching adventures, it's also renowned for ocean kayaking and spelunking (caving), and it is the beginning of the forty-eight-kilometre hike to Cape Scott Provincial Park. You'll need to stay in this magical little community, so you can catch the morning ferry to Sointula and Pulteney Point. Port McNeill boasts a campground, some fine B&Bs, and a hotel.

It's only a forty-minute crossing to Sointula on Malcolm Island. Explore this co-operative-minded village with its museum, craft shops, and colourfully painted houses. To get to the lighthouse, find 1st Street and follow it north. Turn right at Bere Road, then turn left at Pulteney Point Road and follow it directly to the lighthouse. Park in the turnabout near the beach. A ten- to fifteen-minute walk will get you to the light station. Leaving your car in Port McNeill and taking your bicycling over to Malcolm Island (perhaps staying over in Sointula) is really the best way to go.

THE WEIRD Some light keepers, such as Arthur Gurney (Ballenas Island), left his post and went off to war, returning home unscathed. Others, like Robert Lally (Estevan Point), remained home at the station and faced a similar risk of enemy bombardment, though from the open sea. Pulteney Point Lighthouse would play a significant role in two world wars, but in November 1914 the seriousness of that danger first became patently clear. The Victoria *Daily Colonist* carried the following chilling message:

▼ left *New lamp in the cupola.* right *Solar panel for the new light.*

COASTAL LIGHTS ARE EXTINGUISHED.

The Western part of Broughton Strait is closed to navigation.

All vessels, whether north or south-bound, proceeding from Johnstone Strait to Queen Charlotte Sound, or vice versa, must pass through Weyman passage and Backfish Sound. Masters of vessels attempting to pass between Ellen Point and Pulteney Point are liable to be fired upon. The govt. has gained knowledge of hostile ships; all lights at Pulteney Point and Haddington Reef are discontinued as of Saturday, Nov 14.[130]

Germany had been quietly at war with Canada and its Allies since August 1914, but it was unlikely to pose a palpable threat to our isolated, empty northern coast. In fact, in those early months of World War I, it was felt that China and Japan posed a greater threat to our shores than did Germany, even though Japan itself declared war on Germany early on in the conflict.

Britain had been systematically vacating its Esquimalt base since the early 1900s, so when war broke out, that process was simply accelerated. Canada had a navy (the same Department of Marine and Fisheries that oversaw light stations also oversaw the fledgling naval service), but it was real only on paper. British Columbia premier Richard McBride wasted no time in telling the British Press "that British Columbia had been left defenceless by the withdrawal of the Royal Navy."[131] Britain was adamant; the Royal Navy was needed in European waters, so Canada had better get its act together.

By mid-1914, it was known that two German heavy battleships, SMS *Leipzig* and SMS *Nürnberg,* were prowling about in the North Pacific, and German freighters were seen off BC waters, spying on Allied ship movements. Unguarded, the BC coast's vast coalfields, huge fishing fleet, and natural harbours would have been war prizes of incalculable worth. Canada's only battleship, the aging cruiser HMCS *Rainbow*, would, in 1916, become involved in aiding Russia's plan to move billions in gold bullion to Vancouver and Ottawa via Vladivostok, just in case there was a revolution. Besides, submarines would soon be built in secret for the Russian navy at the British Pacific Construction and Engineering Company in Burnaby. With the threat of war looming, Pulteney Point Lighthouse had suddenly become strategically important.

THE NAME Pulteney Point Lighthouse is named after Sir Pulteney Malcolm, who joined the Royal Navy at twenty and quickly rose through the ranks to become an admiral. He served in the Mediterranean and was involved in the pursuit of the French fleet to the West Indies in October 1805. He returned October 24 and just missed joining Admiral Nelson at the Battle of Trafalgar by three days, but provided valuable assistance to many disabled ships. He also saved many Spanish sailors who found themselves blown into the water. Pulteney Malcolm met Napoleon Bonaparte, who said of him in 1816, "Ah, there is a man with a countenance really pleasing, open, intelligent, frank and sincere."[132] In 1846, Captain Gordon of HMS *Cormorant* honoured the life of Admiral Malcolm by naming the point and island after this brilliant and much-loved naval commander.

Prior to the arrival of white settlers, Pulteney Point, Malcolm and Cormorant Islands, and Alert Bay were Kwakwaka'wakw territory. However, an Indigenous legend foretold that the Malcolm Island would one day sink into the sea, so it was never permanently inhabited.[133] In 1900, when a group Finns, unhappy with the hard, labouring life associated with Dunsmuir's mines in Nanaimo, received Ottawa's permission to settle on Malcolm Island and set up a co-operative, they petitioned Ottawa to provide them with a lighthouse. Ottawa complied.

▲ *Caspian tern with supper.*

DESIGN AND CONSTRUCTION   Early in 1905, Colonel William P. Anderson, Canada's superintendent of lighthouses and designer of the famous flying buttress, gave the go-ahead for a series of light stations to be constructed down the length of the Inside Passage. Malcolm Island was at the top of the list. The spit at the western end of the island turned out to be the perfect location. Ships heading south from the expansive Pacific into Queen Charlotte Strait needed a clear warning to the approaches and dangers of the myriad islands and narrowing channels of Broughton Strait, through to Georgia Strait. In May 1905, Anderson appointed contractor George Frost (who built the lighthouses at Lucy Island, Cape Mudge, and Trial Islands) to build a lighthouse at Pulteney Point. It was to be a copy of the light station on Discovery Island.

The original light-station at Pulteney Point was a square wooden two-storey dwelling with a lean-to addition and a short tower and balcony protruding from its roof. The light was a seventh-order dioptric-lens lamp, which stood nearly twelve metres

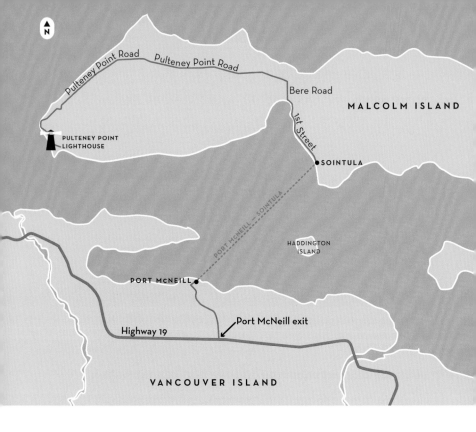

above the water and was visible northwards for some seventeen kilometres.

THE KEEPERS In 1900, Finnish writer and social activist Matti Kurikka was summoned from Australia to British Columbia to lead his countrymen away from Robert Dunsmuir's brutal exploitation of miners in Nanaimo. From there, an opportunity arose to carve out of the wilderness a new community based on Kurikka's utopian and religious ideals. Kurikka became the president of Kalevan Kansa ("people of Kaleva," a figure from Finnish mythology). In 1901, he was joined by countryman August Mäkelä when the British Columbia government granted them land on unsettled Malcolm Island, which became the village of Sointula (meaning "a harmonious place"). Thus, a new experiment in communal socialism began.

But it wouldn't last. Matti Kurikka's notions about strict vegetarianism, the communal rearing of children, free love among the parents, the problems of clearing first-growth timber for arable land, and the inherent difficulties of making ends meet proved too difficult for many. Kurikka left, but not before Mäkelä saved them from imminent collapse.[134]

Within a few years, Sointula boasted some two hundred residents; a sawmill, blacksmith's shop, foundry, and bakery; and the only Finnish-language newspaper in British Columbia. Though the social experiment at Sointula did eventually dissolve, a general store and revised co-operative movement began in 1909 and lasted through to the 1940s. In the early years, August Mäkelä supplemented his income by becoming Pulteney Point's first light keeper.

At first, "Austin McKela" (as he was also known) did a fine job. Beyond keeping the light, he was given a hand-operated foghorn and told to ring it after approaching ships whistled for navigational assistance. Yet the winters on Malcolm Island were damp and cold, and McKela asked Ottawa for a wood stove. The service said no and suggested that that if he desired one he should acquire it himself.[135]

A succession of Finnish keepers kept the light at Pulteney Point until World War II. Along the way, a mechanical foghorn replaced the hand-operated one in 1915, and it was replaced with an compressed-air diaphone in 1931. Following the shelling incident at Estevan Point Lighthouse in 1942, the light at Pulteney Point was once again extinguished. The blackout might have thwarted enemy shipping, but it caused the 1942 grounding of the Alaska steamship *Columbia* on the beach right in front of the light.

The old tower was replaced with a circular reinforced-concrete one in 1943. Pulteney Point Lighthouse is considered a plum of a posting in that the keeper's children could attend the local school and the lighthouse family could interact directly with the warm-hearted residents of Sointula. As of 2014, the station is still manned.

MIKE MITCHELL

24

QUATSINO

LAT 50°26′30″ N, **LONG** 128°01′55″ W

ACCESSIBILITY ❺ Really, Really Hard

GETTING THERE Of all the lighthouses in this book, Quatsino Lighthouse on Kains Island is probably the most difficult to get to. If you are going on your own power, make sure you and your travel companions are serious wilderness aficionados with lots of time, first-class camping gear, and plenty of sea-kayak experience.

It's a long, long drive to Holberg, west of Port Hardy, then another four hours on a logging road to Winter Harbour. After that, it's at least a two-day kayak trip to Kains Island. Travel inshore of Pinnacle and Matthews Islands and watch the weather closely. Post a route and itinerary with local officials.

Better yet, you can take a water taxi from Winter Harbour. Have them take you, drop you off, and pick you up at a specified time, a day or two later. Explore small Kains Island completely and photograph the marine wildlife. The sea lions will astound you.

THE WEIRD When James Sadler replaced Nels Nelson as light keeper in 1915, the supply ship visited Kains Island only once a year. At the time it was still the most isolated of all of the light stations on Vancouver Island. This meant that Sadler had to row some fifteen kilometres (return) to Winter Harbour to get his mail. But that was the least of it. On September 11, 1918, the Victoria *Daily Colonist* reported:

> [Sadler's] wife Catherine had become violently insane from the awful loneliness of the West Coast and two of his four children were in a precarious condition through lack of food. Sadler was found at his post . . . after he had exhausted himself in his efforts to keep his wife from committing suicide.[136]

THE NAME The origin of the name of Kains Island is obscure, though its roots are most likely Aboriginal. However, Scots-Gaelic might have played some distant role, as there used to be quite a few Scotsmen in isolated Quatsino Sound. There's a Kains Island off the coast of Ireland to which many of the Scottish clans who lived on the English/Scottish borderlands were banished after a rebellion in 1603. In that context, the name Kains suggests an independent, if lonely, place. In Gaelic, the word *cain* means "payment in kind," alluding to the redress given to the clans for their uprising.

However, most likely, *Kains* is derivative of an Aboriginal term. In 1906, Robert Stapleton, the manager of the Inverness Cannery supplied this interpretation of the similarly named Kaien Island in Tuck Inlet, near Prince Rupert: "After heavy rains when the current runs swiftly, there are quantities of 'seafoam' which float on the water."[137] The Tsimshian peoples named this phenomenon *kaien*. The same peculiarity occurs at Kains Island in

Quatsino Sound. The white, sticky seafoam can be so thick after a storm that it can easily cover any person standing at the edge of the surf.

The Quatsino First Nation speaks Gut'sala, a dialect of the Kwak'wala language, which is part of the Wakashan language family. In the early 1800s, this once numerous and powerful nation controlled a territory from San Josef Bay to Winter Harbour, but sadly by the early 1900s, the Quatsino population had declined dramatically.

DESIGN AND CONSTRUCTION   With the opening up of Nootka Sound to mining and logging at the turn of the twentieth century, it didn't take long for similar activities to begin in earnest farther north, in Quatsino Sound. Soon, increased shiploads of ore and milled logs travelled down this desolate watercourse, and the inherent dangers of fog, winter seas, and inshore reefs resulted in cries for navigational aids. In 1904, on the southern tip of Kains Island, a small, barren outcropping at the mouth of Quatsino Sound, the federal government constructed a bare platform with room enough for an enclosed cupola which housed a continuous-burning (thirty-one-day) oil lamp. The whole precarious structure cost Ottawa $700. Beyond that, a Mr. G. Jackson, who lived in Winter Harbour, was paid $300 per year, "to keep an eye on it."[138]

In 1910, H.C. Killeen was awarded the contract to construct a proper, more permanent light station on Kains Island on the site of the original platform. Like many others, the lighthouse was built as a square wooden two-storey dwelling with a lamp gallery and railing protruding from its roof. The original Wickham Lamp, which burned for a month without filling, was replaced with a more powerful lensed and mirrored beam. This structure stood for over sixty years. In 1923, a diaphone building was added. In 1977, the wooden station was demolished and a concrete dwelling, foghorn building, and cylindrical tower were built on its spot. That structure remains today.

▲ *Note the impenetrable surf and modern-day helipad.* MIKE MITCHELL

THE KEEPERS Nels Nelson and his wife were Quatsino's first keepers, and they stayed at their post for five years. In December 1913, Mrs. Nelson's brother, Walter Peterson, was visiting his sister from Denmark, when his small skiff capsized inshore. He was just twenty years old. He was buried by Nels on the island, and a stone monument to his brief life now stands over his grave. The Nelsons left Quatsino two years later.

James Sadler replaced Nels Nelson in 1915, but the place turned out to be cruel to him, too. In his first year of service, his wife, Catherine, gave birth to their second child in Quatsino Village, and James and his one-year-old son accompanied her, even though James was not allowed to desert his station under any circumstances. The necessity of James keeping his job, combined with the unpredictability of the vicious winds and storms and the never-ending workload, forced Catherine to deliver their third child at the lighthouse itself. Worse, getting through the breakers in a small skiff with a month's load of supplies nearly cost James his life several times. When, in 1918, Catherine learned that her younger brother had died in World War I, she snapped. James flew the station's ensign upside-down for eight days before the family was finally rescued. His beloved Catherine was committed to an insane asylum and never fully recovered.

It was the danger, the desolation, and the terrible wages that kept the turnover of Quatsino Lighthouse keepers so high in the 1920s. Most stayed for just one year.

In 1925, Jesse and Syd Warren and their seven daughters arrived. It was they who discovered the white-post marker in the woods that most, until then, believed was only some sort of navigational day marker for approaching boats. Nearby, they found the 1913 grave and stone monument of young Walter Peterson. It read:

Walter Peterson
Born at Copenhagen
Aug 13, 1893
Died at Quatsino
Dec 18, 1913

On October 23, 1929, after just beginning his fourth year as light keeper, Sydney Warren drowned in front of his family when an inshore breaker capsized his skiff.

When light keeper Clarence Carver and his wife, Evelyn, had their son, Ray, at Kains Island in the 1930s, the doctor at Port Alice strongly suggested the boy receive fresh milk. So Clarence brought a goat to the lighthouse thinking it would eat anything and require little care. Unfortunately, the goat didn't come when called, and it had a penchant for climbing cliffs where humans couldn't go. So the goat-milk idea was a bust, and Ray drank canned condensed milk for most of his youth.[139]

In 1998, assistant light keeper Paul Hollyoak arrived at Kains Island. His wife, a teacher, home-schooled the five children. They and others all reported seeing the ghost of Walter Peterson walking

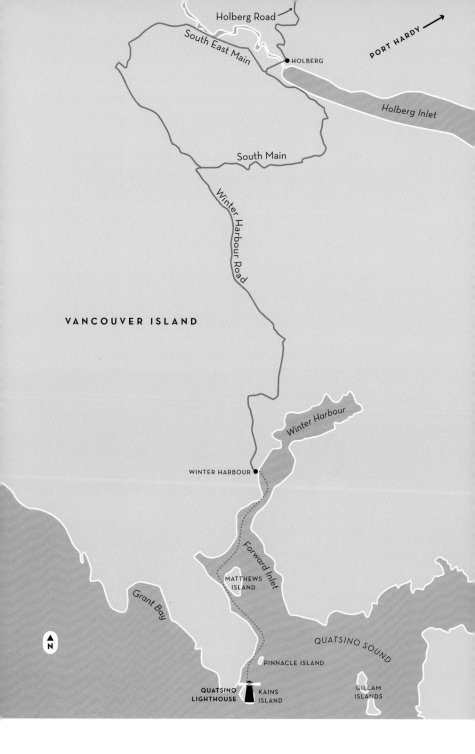

Holberg Road

South East Main

PORT HARDY

HOLBERG

Holberg Inlet

South Main

Winter Harbour Road

VANCOUVER ISLAND

Winter Harbour

WINTER HARBOUR

Forward Inlet

MATTHEWS ISLAND

Grant Bay

QUATSINO SOUND

N

PINNACLE ISLAND

GILLAM ISLANDS

QUATSINO LIGHTHOUSE

KAINS ISLAND

North Vancouver Island **197**

in the woods. Kains Island, perhaps more than most other light stations on Vancouver Island's outer coast, had its share of ghosts.

In 2006, light keeper C. Rene Ammundsen wrote:

Human visitors tend to arrive in herds. When a helicopter is headed our way, all wishing this destination hop on. Last week, Grandma led the way, but not by chopper. She arrived from Winter Harbour in an 18ft aluminum water-taxi. She had 10 hens under one arm and boxes of plants under the other.

One way or another, the sea brings most of our visitors and sometimes it makes them stay. As it surges and ebbs it brings an ever-changing array of life. The variety never ceases to amaze us.[140]

▼ *"Now let me show you how to really catch a salmon."*

MIKE MITCHELL

25

CAPE SCOTT

LAT 50°46'53" N, **LONG** 128°25'37" W

ACCESSIBILITY ❺ Really, Really Hard

GETTING THERE Not for inexperienced hikers, there is a forty-eight-kilometre round-trip trail through Cape Scott Provincial Park to the lighthouse. It's flat and well maintained, but the area is renowned for extreme cold and wet weather conditions, even in summer. If you seek the reward of isolated, crescent-shaped white sandy beaches and spectacular wildlife, and if you are experienced and athletic, this multi-day hike is for you. There are, however, two easier ways to get there, so read on.

Drive north on Vancouver Island Highway 19 beyond Port McNeill. Just south of Port Hardy watch for Holberg Road. Take Holberg Road and travel forty-five kilometres to Holberg. Continue on St. Joseph Main and follow the Cape Scott Provincial Park signposts. The Cape Scott/San Josef Bay trailhead is at the end of San Josef Main, about eighteen kilometres from Holberg or sixty-five kiloetres from Highway 19. The park is a completely hike-in recreational area.

From the trailhead, there are trails to Hansen Lagoon, Fisherman Bay, Nissen Bight, Nels Bight, and Guise Bay. One trail goes west to San Josef Bay (2.5 kilometres), where there is rudimentary camping. Here the trail turns north past the remains of the Danish settlement and on to Nels Bight (twelve kilometres). Another, the North Coast Trail, runs along the beaches in Nissen Bight, then joins the original Cape Scott Trail. Once you get to Nels Bight, the Cape Scott Lighthouse is on Department of National Defence land and is another 6.5 kilometres away. This part of the trail is not maintained, so be mindful of deadfall, mud, and slippery rotting planks on whatever is left of the boardwalks. The round-trip hike back to the trailhead is approximately forty-eight kilometres, and will naturally take several days.

There is camping at Eric Lake (three kilometres in), Nels Bight (nineteen kilometres in), and Guise Bay (twenty-one kilometres in). Do carry high-top rubber boots, gators, as well as proper hiking boots, complete raingear, a water maker, a rain-fly for your tent, a VHF radio, and rope for hauling food up into trees beyond the reach of bears and other scavengers.

Remember, you are on the rain coast and in the wettest part of Canada. Don't forget maps (topographic map #1021/09 and hydrographic chart #3624 "Cape Cook to Cape Scott" are the best), and carry up-to-date tide and current tables. Read widely and plan carefully. Train by carrying bricks in your packsack each evening around your block for two months before you leave—taunting neighbours be damned.

Another way is to leave your car in Port Hardy and catch the North Coast Trail bus, which takes ten passengers to the trailhead and operates from May 1 to September 15. Reservations are required. The North Coast Trail office in Port Hardy also runs a water-taxi service to Shushartie Bay and beyond.

Cape Scott Provincial Park is a remote, 22,000-hectare natural paradise, rich in first-growth cedar and Sitka spruce, intertidal beaches with sandhill cranes, shellfish, oystercatchers, and mist-enshrouded beaches with plovers, snipes, wolves, cougars, and prowling bears. Keep in mind as the rain drips from the end of your nose, that getting to the Cape Scott Lighthouse is more about the journey and less about the destination.

THE WEIRD Originally constructed in 1960, the Cape Scott Lighthouse is one of the very last lighthouses to be built on Canada's west coast. In June 1975, a monthly grocery run was being made by the CCGS *Sir James Douglas* to the Cape Scott Lighthouse. As was the procedure, the mothership stood off while supplies were unloaded into one of the ship's lifeboats for the run closer inshore. There, up a rock cut, a hook on a highline cable would grasp the goods in a webbed-rope basket and transfer them high over the surf to shore. On the way into the cut, ocean swells alternately lifted and dropped the workboat as its slow-throbbing engine resolutely powered it closer to shore. Suddenly one huge swell caught the boat sideways and threw it, crew included, up onto a nearby rock shelf. As the swell withdrew, the boat rolled over, spilling its loads down the rocks and

The ever-stealthy and alert Great Blue heron.

into the foaming sea. The crew had only enough time to see another swell approaching and hung onto the boat's gunwales for dear life. The boat was lifted up again and this time deposited, right side up, back into the water, its propeller still turning. Afloat, though full of water, the pumps were started and the stunned and the lucky crew made their way back to the mothership for yet another load. That was one crapshoot that Nature didn't win.[141]

THE NAME Cape Scott is named after David Scott, a merchant from Mumbai, who in 1786 was a main financial backer of a trading expedition to this part of the world. This two-vessel voyage under the command of James Strange was only the second expedition ever to Nootka and to points farther north. The taking of sea otter pelts, which were readily available from local Aboriginals, established the feasibility of ongoing trade with the Northwest Coast.

From 1897 to 1909, a Danish-American community was established at the end of Hansen Lagoon on the Cape Scott Peninsula. Largely from Minnesota, Iowa, Nebraska, and North Dakota, the group of about sixty people planned to fish and farm until a government-promised road to San Josef and on to Holberg gave them access to markets for wider trade and commerce. The government reneged on their promise, and the settlers were forced to abandon their houses to work in logging and mining camps farther down the sounds of the outer coast.

In 1913, a second group of would-be pioneers, numbering over one thousand, inhabited the vacated houses of the original Danish settlement and began a similar experiment. It, too, failed due to the inhospitable weather conditions, infighting, and transportation problems. The outbreak of World War I saw the region depopulated completely until the Department of National Defence set up a radar station at Cape Scott in 1942, as part of the Allied war effort to provide listening posts for possible Japanese air attacks on the BC coast. The radar station at Cape Scott was a major military undertaking and had a wooden corduroy-road built to the end of the peninsula. There were barracks for fifty men, a mess hall, a hospital, a diesel-generating station, and a state-of-the-art operations building.

Three separate First Nation groups had lived in the Cape Scott area for centuries before the arrival of a Europeans. In the mid-1850s they amalgamated with the First Nations of Quatsino Sound and became known collectively as the Nahwitti.

DESIGN AND CONSTRUCTION Right up until the 1920s, far beyond Quatsino Sound to the very northern tip of Vancouver Island, all was dark. There was a light on Triangle Island some thirty kilometres northwest of Cape Scott out in the open Pacific, but nobody could see it. It was placed too high on the island's summit and was obscured by the continual fog that hovered beneath it. When the second Danish settlement left Cape Scott in the late 1920s, the stake light and lantern they had placed at the Cape's tip left with them. All was dark once again.

Then in the 1950s, the Canadian mining company and aluminum manufacturer Alcan created Kitimat, their company township on the north coast. To do it they had to dam the Nechako River and run a new watercourse seventeen kilometres under a mountain to their generating station at Kemano. Aluminum production demands great amounts of electricity! That brought ships, which in turn brought the need for the last three lighthouses to be built on BC's coast: Chatham Point, Bonilla Island, and Cape Scott.

The first tower at Cape Scott was begun in 1959. It sits on the old concrete base of the radar tower left by the military in 1945. The station's barracks became the machine room for the twin diesel engines that gave the lighthouse electricity and ran a compressed-air apparatus for the diaphone foghorn. The actual horns were housed in a smaller hut much nearer the shore, requiring the construction of an elevated walkway across a surge channel to access it.

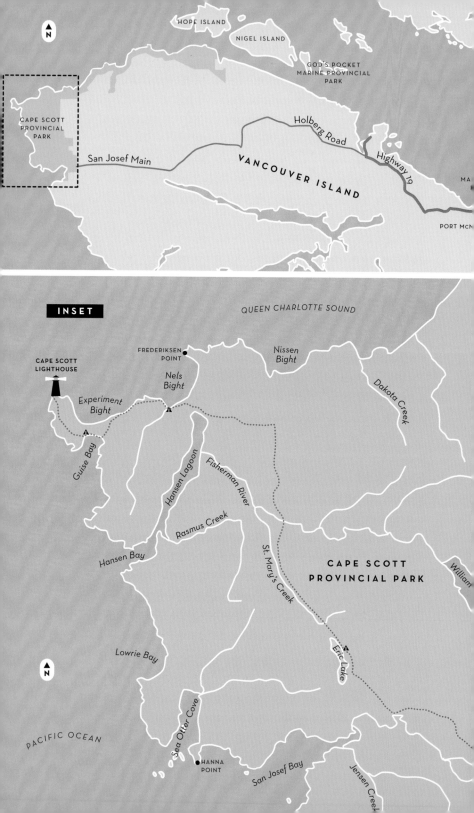

In 1981, the original tower was replaced with an open skeleton steel tower containing a powerful, DCB-36 electric beacon.

THE KEEPERS William Gardner, Cape Scott's first keeper, who lit the light in October 1960, only had to move "around the corner" from Kains Island in Quatsino Sound. Living at Quatsino, Gardner understood isolation and was a shoo-in for the job at Cape Scott.

The most recent keeper, Harvey Humchitt, and his assistant keeper, Todd Maliszewski, were posted to the Cape Scott Lighthouse in 2003. They knew the old days of the keepers and admitted that even with all of today's lighthouse technology, life on the stations still tests the soul. Humchitt remembered a storm at Cape Scott in 2005 with hurricane-force winds "that sent ocean spray over the lighthouse some 200 feet above the water, with ping-pong-sized hail, and 600 cm. of rain in 2½ days."[142] At times like these during frequent winter storms, even the helicopters can't fly, so self-sufficiency is still paramount.

A self-styled greenhouse and garden provide all the fresh produce that the monthly airlift does not bring. The helicopter supplies the keepers and their families with frozen meat, staples, diesel fuel, gasoline, backup batteries, and replacement equipment necessary for the light. The recyclables are flown out to Victoria; everything else is composted. Humchitt appreciates the almost maintenance-free bulbs for the electric light, which replaced the old wick lamps, but he is more taken by the genius and artistry of the nineteenth-century Fresnel lens, "which can magnify the output of a single 30 watt bulb and have it seen some 30 miles away."[143] The eight-thousand-litre fuel tank lasts only seven months, and if storms prevent helicopters from flying, resourcefulness must win the day. In times like these, both Humchitt and Maliszewski become paranoid about sickness. Humchitt, strangely, worries about scurvy, Maliszewski about appendicitis.[144] The Cape Scott Lighthouse is one of the few that is still manned today.

GLOSSARY

acetylene When highly flammable pressurized acetylene gas is passed through an electric arc, a largely smoke-free flame is the result. Canadian Thomas Wilson discovered the acetylene light in 1892 and began manufacturing such lamps. Acetylene lamps required little maintenance.

aerial high-line cable Since lighthouses are often a considerable height and distance from the shore where supply ships would leave oil, coal, food, and other goods monthly, some lighthouses were equipped with a high-line cable running from the lighthouse to the shore. The cable allowed for a rope sling, or basket, or even a small "car," to move supplies up to the light station.

ALN (automated listening network) A VHF/UHF telephone network that was begun in the 1970s to communicate with and control automated lighthouses on the Pacific Coast.

Argand lamps François Argand invented the Argand lamp in 1783. The fuel tube of an Argand lamp is holed, allowing a circular wick to draw in great quantities of air, producing an intense flame that was low in soot. Combined with mirrors, the Argand lamp was the brightest light of its time.

beacon A beacon is a small, unmanned, lighted or unlighted signal, permanently attached to the earth's surface, as in the port hand day beacon at the entrance to Silva Bay on Gabriola Island.

bell buoy Where fixed lights and/or foghorns were impracticable, this aid to navigation was an anchored buoy, whose clappers activated its bell by wave action. There is a bell buoy off Spanish Banks and the southern entrance of English Bay in Vancouver.

bulls-eye lens Fresnel lenses often had two or more convex panels called bull's eyes. When rotated, the light seemed to flash intermittently. Clamshell lenses had two bulls-eye lenses.

Chance Brothers Hailing from Birmingham, England, the Chance Brothers were the renowned manufacturers of Fresnel prismatic lenses. They soon eclipsed the French Letourneau Company, the German Weuke Company, and Macbeth-Evans of America, becoming, by 1888, the industry standard. Chance Brothers also made clockwork drives to rotate heavy lens systems.

cupola The usually domed cover that protected the lamp housing from the elements.

elevation The height of the light tower to the lamp room. The actual beam from the lamp is usually higher, and it sends out its light waves in a narrow beam called the focal plane. The curve of the earth's surface limits how far the light beam will reach, so the number given as the focal plane of a particular light indicates to a mariner the light's range or distance. A light beam with a focal plane of forty-five metres, for example, can be seen for up to twenty nautical miles.

fixed light beam Many light sources are seen to flash or shine intermittently. A fixed light source shines continuously. This characteristic helps distinguish it from other lights.

flashing light beam This is a light source that seems to go on and off at regular intervals. Now electric switches accomplish that task. Earlier lighthouses had panels, or baffles, that rotated around the light, giving the impression of an intermittent light flash. Or the bulls-eye lens housing itself rotated around the light. Characteristically different flashing intervals for each and every lighthouse indicated its geographic position.

focal plane The height of the light beam above the sea.

fog signals This could be a bell, a trumpet, a cannon, a whistle, compressed steam, or compressed air that blew through a trumpet-like horn called a diaphone. Today's foghorns are usually electric.

Fresnel lens A lens system that uses prisms (rather than a reflective mirror) to concentrate light into a single powerful beam. An ordering system classified the Fresnel lens's size (and hence its brightness). A first-order Fresnel lens was the brightest (two metres in diameter). A seventh-order Fresnel lens was much dimmer and smaller than the size of a basketball hoop. "D1"=brightest; D7=dimmest. (D stands for diopter.)

gallery This is the circular walkway around the outside of the cupola at the top of a lighthouse, which holds the lamp. It is necessary because ocean spray, bits of plants, insects, and fish often hit the lamp housing during storms. Birds, too, are often drawn into the light beam and killed against the glass. Light keepers need a walkway to get at and clean the outside of the lamp room's windows.

hyper-radial lenses These lens systems were even larger than the massive, first-order Fresnel lenses. Some lenses in hyper-radial systems could be 3.6 metres in diameter. (A first-order Fresnel was only two metres.)

lamp and reflector systems Before the invention of the Fresnel lens, a mirror was used to concentrate the light beam. A catoptric system used reflecting mirrors to intensify the light. A catadioptric system used lenses and mirrors to intensify the light beam. It burned more oil than a dioptric system, which refracted light by lenses and prisms. By 1890, the dioptric system, the brightest, became the norm in enhancing a light beam's focal plane.

light lists Hydrographic Services (Canada) published these documents annually. They contained the location and precise flashing characteristics of a given lighthouse for a specified area of coast. This list enabled a mariner to correctly identify a lighthouse beam and its exact location. Then by locating that lighthouse on a chart, a bearing or two would establish his own ship's location on that chart.

lightships Some lamps are placed high in the mast of a ship, anchored over a certain spot, rather than on a shoreside station. The Sand Heads Lighthouse, seawards of Vancouver International Airport at the mouth of the Fraser River, used to be a lightship.

mercury baths To minimize the friction of heavy rotating-lens systems, many lens housings were floated on small mercury balls placed in a shallow tub. Highly dangerous, such baths resulted in some light keepers getting mercury poisoning. Rollers or chariots of wheel assemblies replaced the mercury baths when its poisonous nature became known.

occulting lights A lighthouse lamp can be made to appear flashing in many ways. An electric switch is one. Rotating panels of varying widths, spaced regularly around the light, created a specific duration of a light's flash. An occulting light is one whose total duration of light is longer than the total duration of darkness. An occulting light is more on than off (as opposed to isophase lights, which alternate equal durations of light and darkness).

oil houses Early lighthouses used whale oil, coal oil, kerosene, and other oils to light the lamps in their towers. Initially kept in the keeper's dwelling, the oil containers occasionally caused disastrous fires, so they were later stored in a separate building, or oil house.

range lights These are two lights, which, when aligned vertically together, keep a vessel within a safe, narrow navigable channel. In range lights, the rear range-light is always higher (and farther from the water) than the front range light. If the range lights are not aligned vertically, the helmsman must steer in the opposite direction to bring the lights back into vertical alignment once again. Porlier Pass Lighthouse on Race Point and the rear light at Virago Point are fine examples of local range lights.[145]

skeleton steel tower This is a light tower made of steel or aluminum and is open to the elements. There is a steel light tower on Flora Island off Hornby Island and at East Point on Saturna Island.

vega lights These are fully automated, usually rotating, electric halogen lamps placed in waterproof containers as beacons. Very remote locations favour vega lights today.

APPENDIX

GPS (Global Positioning System) co-ordinates for the lighthouses covered in this book

Sheringham Point: *lat 48.3768, long -123.921*

Race Rocks: *lat 48.2983, long -123.53171*

Fisgard: *lat 48.43039, long -123.44757*

Trial Islands: *lat 48.3951, long -123.3050*

Discovery Island: *lat 48.4245, long -123.2255*

Fiddle Reef: *lat 48.4329, long -123.2258*

East Point: *lat 48.7830, long -123.0454*

Active Pass: *lat 48.8733, long -123.2915*

Portlock Point: *lat 48.8278, long -123.3518*

Porlier Pass: *lat 49.0129, long -123.5859*

Entrance Island: *lat 49.2091, long -123.8086*

Ballenas Islands: *lat 49.3505, long -124.16022*

Sisters Islets: *lat 49.4867, long -124.43477*

Chrome Island: *lat 49.4721, long -124.68519*

Cape Mudge: *lat 49.9985, long -125.19561*

Carmanah Point: *lat 48.6115, long -124.75133*

Pachena Point: *lat 48.7220, long -125.09754*

Cape Beale: *lat 48.7864, long -125.2155*

Amphitrite Point: *lat 48.9203, long -125.5443*

Lennard Island: *lat 49.1104, long -125.92352*

Estevan Point: *lat 49.3829, long -126.54402*

Nootka: *lat 49.5926, long -126.615389*

Pulteney Point: *lat 50.6305, long -127.155257*

Quatsino: *lat 50.4411, long -128.03244*

Cape Scott: *lat 50.7825, long -128.425778*

ACKNOWLEDGEMENTS

The original concept for this book came from the members of the Sheringham Point Lighthouse Preservation Society, whose aim since 2003 has been to preserve the buildings, grounds, and history of the Sheringham Point Lighthouse in Shirley, British Columbia. Since its inception, the society has chronicled the unique stories of Sheringham Point's light keepers, their families, and the mariners whom they served—and it is working still to restore the lighthouse and its outbuildings to their original operating status, all within the scope of a surrounding community park.

We would like to acknowledge the dedication of Terri Alcock, Elanie Bruton, Sharon Kerrigan-Bruton, Michael Galizio, Rebecca Quinn, the late Jim Ryan, Noel Taylor, and the service of the Canadian Coast Guard and Fisheries and Oceans Canada.

The idea expanded, in the course of much discussion among the three of us, to become an explorer's guidebook and celebration of twenty-five major island lighthouses in southwestern British Columbia. Others who helped immeasurably were Noel Havers, the MV *Uchuck III* Organization, Elida Peers, John Gellard, and Sonja Dönnecke.

Without publisher Rodger Touchie's confidence in us, designer Jacqui Thomas's creative brilliance, and editor Lara Kordic's eagle eye, we would have nothing. Thank you, all.

Peter Johnson
John Walls
Richard Paddle

NOTES

1.   Rudyard Kipling, *The Collected Poems of Rudyard Kipling* (London: Wordsworth Editions, 1989), 173.

2.   Basil Lubbock, *The Last of the Windjammers* (Glasgow: Brown, Son & Ferguson, 1935), 2:18.

3.   Roland Paxton, *Dynasty of Engineers: The Stevensons and the Bell Rock* (Edinburgh: Northern Lighthouse Heritage Trust, 2011), 35.

4.   Department of Marine and Fisheries, Sec. III, A 25-1, "Admission and Conduct of Keepers, 1869," in Normand Lafrenière, *Lightkeeping on the St. Lawrence: The End of an Era* (Toronto: Dundurn Press, 1996), 41.

5.   Ibid.

6.   Ibid.

7.   Ibid., 44–45.

8.   "Quatsino (Kains Island), BC," lighthousefriends.com/light.asp?ID=1195.

9.   See the appendix to Donald Graham's *Keepers of the Light: A History of British Columbia's Lighthouses and Their Keepers* (Madeira Park, BC: Harbour Publishing, 1985). See also, Donald Graham, *Lights of the Inside Passage: A History of British Columbia's Lighthouses and Their Keepers* (Madeira Park, BC: Harbour Publishing, 1985).

10.   "Pacheenaht," Historica Canada, blog, thecanadianencyclopedia.ca/en/article/pacheenaht/.

11.   John Walbran, *British Columbia Coast Names: Their Origin and History* (Vancouver: Douglas & McIntyre, 1971), 456, previously published as *British Columbia Coast Names* (Ottawa: Government Printing Bureau, 1909).

12.   Interview with Elida Peers, Sooke, British Columbia, April 14, 2014.

13.   Rebecca Quinn, *A History of the Sheringham Point Lighthouse* (Victoria: Sheringham Point Lighthouse Preservation Society, 2004), 4.

14.   Ibid.

15.   "Sheringham Point Lighthouse," lighthousefriends.com/light.asp?ID=1103.

16.   Ibid.

17.   Interview with Sharon Kerrigan Bruton, daughter of Sheringham light keeper James Bruton, December 18, 2014.

18.   Quinn, *A History of the Sheringham Point Lighthouse*, 5.

19.   Interview with Sharon Kerrigan Bruton, December 16, 2014.

20.   Ibid.

21.   Ibid.

22.   "Early History of the Light Station–Part 2," Race Rocks Ecological Reserve, racerocks.ca/wp/2007/02/08/.

23.   Alexander Findlay, *Sailing Directions for the North Pacific Ocean* (London: Richard Holmes and Co., 1870), 318.

24.   Walbran, *British Columbia Coast Names,* 412.

25.   "Race Rocks Lighthouse," metchosinmuseum.ca/race-rocks-lighthouse.

26.   Andrew Ritchie, letter to Garry Fletcher, education director at Lester B. Pearson College, 2003.

27.   Walbran, *British Columbia Coast Names*, 179.

28.   "Fisgard Lighthouse," members.shaw.ca/rkcampbell/fisgard/fisgard.htm.

29.   Ibid.

30.   Graham, *Keepers of the Light,* 17.

31. "Fisgard Lighthouse," members.shaw.ca/rkcampbell/fisgard/fisgard.htm.

32. *Daily Colonist*, January 29, 1869, 3.

33. Ibid., 3.

34. Walbran, *British Columbia Coast Names*, 169.

35. Graham, *Keepers of the Light,* 115.

36. Ibid., 116.

37. Ibid.

38. Ibid.,117.

39. Chris Jaksa and Lynn Tanod, *Guiding Lights: BC's Lighthouses and Their Keepers* (Madeira Park, BC: Harbour Publishing, 1998), 22.

40. Patricia Jordan, "Trial Islands Lighthouse," *West Coast Living,* July 21, 2013.

41. "Five Kayakers Rescued off Trial Island," *Kayak Yak,* June 8, 2009, 3.

42. Bill Wolferstan, *Cruising Guide to the Gulf Islands,* Vol. I (Vancouver: Pacific Yachting /Interpress Publications, 1976), 89.

43. *Daily Colonist*, December 11, 1897, 3.

44. Walbran, *British Columbia Coast Names*, 143.

45. Wolferstan, *Cruising Guide to the Gulf Islands*, Vol. I, 219.

46. Ibid., 89.

47. "Surviving on Fiddle Reef Lighthouse c. 1950s," lighthousememories.ca.

48. *Daily Colonist*, March 2, 1888, 3.

49. Graham, *Lights of the Inside Passage,* 26.

50. Ibid., 29.

51. "Government of Canada Designates First Two Heritage Lighthouses in British Columbia," CNW, newswire.ca/en/story/1172015/government-of-canada-designates-first-two-heritage-lighthouses-in-british-columbia.

52. Walbran, *British Columbia Coast Names*, 205.

53. Ibid., 11.

54. Marie Elliott, "Georgeson, Henry (Scotty)," *Dictionary of Canadian Biography* (Toronto: University of Toronto Press, 2005), 418.

55. *Vancouver Sun*, August 12, 1970, 3.

56. *Gulf Islands Driftwood*, August 15, 1979, 1.

57. Walbran, *British Columbia Coast Names*, 398.

58. Chris Arnett, "An Introduction to First Nations' History in the Gulf Islands," Saltspringislandarchives.com/firstnations.

59. Graham, *Lights of the Inside Passage*, 43.

60. Denice Goudie, "Porlier Pass Lighthouse, 1949–1965," lighthousememories.ca/2011/11/27/porlier-pass-lighthouse-1949-1965/.

61. Donald Graham, *Lights of the Inside Passage*, 82.

62. Ibid., 92.

63. Mary and Ted Bentley, *Gabriola: Petroglyph Island* (Victoria: Sono Nis Press, 1981).

64. Peter Johnson, *Glyphs and Gallows: The Rock Art of Clo-oose and the Wreck of the John Bright* (Victoria: Heritage House, 1999), 114.

65. *Times Colonist*, February 9, 2011, 3.

66. "Entrance Island, BC," lighthousefriends.com/light.asp?ID=1105.

67. Ibid.

68. Ibid.

69. *Times Colonist*, August 25, 2014, 3.

70. Wolferstan, *Cruising Guide to the Gulf Islands,* 153.

71. Graham, *Lights of the Inside Passage*, 102.

72. "Ballenas Islands, BC," lighthousefriends.com/light.asp?ID=1185.

73. Graham, *Lights of the Inside Passage*, 78.

74. Chris Jaksa and Lynn Tanod, *Guiding Lights,*102.

75. Islands Trust Executive Committee, "Proposed Plan for Ballenas-Winchelsea Land Use Bylaw 28," 2013, islandstrust.bc.ca.

76. "Sisters Islets, BC," lighthousefriends.com/light.asp?ID=1186.

77. Graham, *Lights of the Inside Passage*, 56.

78. Ibid., 60.

79. "Chrome Island, BC," lighthousefriends.com/light.asp?ID=1187.

80. Walbran, *British Columbia Coast Names*, 536.

81. "Comox," hellobc.com/comox/culture-history.aspx.

82. *The Daily Colonist*, December 19, 1900, 6.

83. Pamela Smyth, "Saving Lives Part of the Job on Chrome Island," *Oceanside Star*, August 12, 2010.

84. Interview with Elanie and Sharon Bruton, October 16, 2014.

85. Ibid.

86. Annie York, Richard Daly, and Chris Arnett, *They Write Their Dreams on the Rock Forever: Rock Writings in the Stein River Valley of British Columbia* (Vancouver: Talonbooks, 1993).

87. Ibid., 223–26. See also, Peter Johnson, *Glyphs and Gallows*, 113, 226.

88. George Vancouver, *A Voyage of Discovery to the North Pacific and Around the World* (Amsterdam: Da Capo Press, 1967), notes 32, 33.

89. Graham, *Lights of the Inside Passage*, 64.

90. Ibid., 67.

91. Walbran, *British Columbia Coast Names*, 57.

92. Ibid., 82.

93. *Daily Colonist*, March 13, 1892, 6.

94. Ibid., August 20, 1892.

95. "Carmanah Point, BC," lighthousefriends.com/light.asp?ID=1201.

96. Donald Graham, *Keepers of the Light,* 146. See also the *Daily Colonist*, October 20, 1910, p. 3, which reported that "700 lives and millions of dollars have been lost in that vicinity through wrecks due to fog."

97. R. Bruce Scott, *Breakers Ahead! A History of Shipwrecks on the Graveyard of the Pacific* (Sidney, BC: Review Publishing, 1970).

98. Ibid., 37–97, 160.

99. G.P. Akrigg and Helen Akrigg, *British Columbia Place Names* (Victoria: Sono Nis Press, 1986), 287.

100. Graham, *Keepers of the Light*, 180.

101. *Daily Colonist,* January 15, 1919, 3i.

102. Walbran, *British Columbia Coast Names*, 39.

103. "Cape Beale, BC," http://www.lighthousefriends.com/light.asp?ID=1199.

104. Ibid.

105. Donald Graham, *Keepers of the Light*, 34.

106. Jaksa and Tanod, *Guiding Lights,* 48.

107. *Daily Colonist*, December 29, 1905, 1.

108. Ibid., 3.

109. "Amphitrite Point, BC," lighthousefriends.com/light.asp?ID=1104.

110. Walbran, *British Columbia Coast Names*, 304.

111. Ibid., 483.

112. Graham, *Keepers of the Light*, 153.

113. Ibid., 159, 162.

114. Interview with Sharon and Elanie Bruton, Metchosin, British Columbia, October 16, 2014.

115. Beverly Schaffer, *Beautiful Lennard Island*, documentary (Ottawa: National Film Board of Canada, 1977).

116. *The Edmonton Journal*, April 2, 2004, 3.

117. *Hesquiat Peninsula, Clayoquot Biosphere's Northern Fringe*, brochure, env.gov.bc.ca/parks.

118. B. Roberts and R. Jones, *Pacific Northwest Lighthouses: Oregon, Washington, Alaska and British Columbia* (Old Saybrook, CT: Pequot Press, 1996), 65.

119. *Daily Colonist*, February 16, 1910, 3.

120. *Daily Colonist*, December 8, 1918, 3.

121. *Daily Colonist*, August 8, 1909, 8.

122. "Lighthouse History –30– Estevan Point (1907-06-16 to 1912-04-14)," lighthousememories.ca/2011/12/01/lighthouse-history-30-estevan-point-1907-06-15-to-1907-07-27/.

123. *Daily Colonist*, December 8, 1908, 9.

124. Brian Peter White, *The Settlement of Nootka Sound: It's Distributional Morphology, 1900–1970*, unpublished master's thesis (Vancouver: Simon Fraser university, 1969), 24–28.

125. Ibid., 27.

126. *Daily Colonist*, January 23, 1906, 3.

127. Donald Graham, *Keepers of the Light*, 244.

128. *Campbell River Courier Islander*, March 19, 2014, 3.

129. Daniel Wood, "Light at the Edge of the World," *Westworld*, spring 2012, 30.

130. *Daily Colonist*, November 17, 1914 (n.p.).

131. Greg Dickson and Mark Forsythe, *From the West Coast to the Western Front: British Columbians and the Great War* (Madeira Park, BC: Harbour Publishing, 2014), 55.

132. Walbran, *British Columbia Coast Names*, 316.

133. "Pulteney Point, BC," lighthousefriends.com/light.asp?ID=1190.

134. *Campbell River Mirror*, May 29, 2014, 1.

135. Graham, *Lights of the Inside Passage*, 113.

136. *Daily Colonist*, September 11, 1918, 3.

137. Walbran, *British Columbia Coast Names*, 276.

138. "Quatsino (Kains Island), BC," lighthousefriends.com/light.asp?ID=1195.

139. "Life on Kains Island 1933–44," lighthousememories.ca/?s=kain+island.

140. C. Rene Ammundsen, "Visitors. Some Come. Some go. Some Stay." This and That, blog, fogwhistle.ca/thisandthat/visitors.htm.

141. "Cape Scott Lighthouse Today," lighthousememories.ca/2011/07/20/cape-scott-lighthouse/.

142. Graham Chandler, "On Cape Scott Keepers," *Legion Magazine*, Jan/Feb 2007, 17.

143. Ibid.

144. Ibid.

145. See Ray Jones, *The Lighthouse Encyclopedia: The Definitive Reference* (Guilford, CT.: 2004), 54–130.

INDEX

Page numbers in italics refer to maps

Active Pass, 79, 82–83, 85–92, 96
Allison, Francis Logan and family, 103–105
SS *Alpha*, 127
Ammundsen, C. Rene, 198
Amphitrite Point, 158–163
Anderson, William P., 36, 175, 180, 189
architecture, 24–25; flying buttresses, 36, 175, 189; steel, 80, 84, 209
Arden, Eustace, 35, 37–38
Argand, François, 22
Argand lamps, 22, 206
Argyle, T., 46–47

Ballenas Islands, 112–117, 119–120, 126
Bamfield, 144, *149*
BC Ferries, 18, 91–92, 180; routes, 85, *91*, 106, *111*, *129*, *135*, *190*
beacon, 48, 72, 76, 84, 105, 206
Beaumont, Ernest Geoffrey, 70
bell buoy, 112, 206
Bevis, William and family, 54
bicycle tours, 100, 131, 186
Blanshard, Benjamin and family, 120–121
boats, charter, 57, 172, 178–179
Bonilla Island, 203
Bonilla Point, 138, *140*
Borgens, Glenn, 107
Brand, Norbie, 157
Brinn, Richard, 68–69
Brown, Henry Edward and family, 101
Brown, William and family, 114–115

Bruton, James (Jim) and family, 38–40, 41, 128–129, 166, 169
Buckholtz, Otto, 176

Campbell River, 131, *135*
Canada Department of Marine and Fisheries, 26, 54, 187; and automation, 64; bomb shelters, 38; and wages, 97, 142
Canada Department of National Defence, 202–203
Canadian Coast Guard, 48, 64, 99, 111, 157, 162, 163, 169
Cape Beale, 137, 138, 143, 148, 151–157
Cape Mudge, 126, 131–136
Cape Scott, 185, 199–205
Carmanah Point, 137–143, 147
Carr, Emily, 183
Carver, Clarence and family, 196
Chance Brothers, 24, 45, 53, 61, 69, 148, 167, 207
Chrome Island, 119, 124–130
Clark, Edwin, 35, 36, 38
Clark, M.G. and family, 109–110
Colquhoun, Iain, 64
communication: and automation, 206; methods, 140, 147; radio-telegraphy, 48, 148
Cormack, William, 56
Cox, Emmanuel and family, 156–157
CPR ships, 90, 139, 182
Croft, Mary Ann, 69–70

Dare, Joseph, 54
Davidson, John and family, 134–136
Davies, George and family, 43, 45–46, 54

Daykin, W.P. (William) and
family, 139–142
Denman Island, 124, *129*
Dickman, Meredith, 64
Discovery Island, 48, 65–71, 74,
189
Dondale, Samuel, 62, 64
Doney, John, 128
Doyle, Kathy, 64

East Point, 78–84, 209
Entrance Island, 106–111
Esquimalt Harbour, 45, 51–52, *55*,
59, 187
Estevan Point, 36, 38, 148,
171–177

Fiddle Reef, 72–77
Fisgard, 45, 50–56, 84
Fish, Tom, 183
fog signals: and duties, 28,
120–121; hand-operated, 19, 61,
89, 96; types, 83–84, 84, 207
Fort Rodd Hill, 50–56
Fraser, James, 161, 163
Fresnel, Augustin, 24
Fresnel lens, 24, 207–208
Friendly Cove, 178–179, 181, 182
Frost, George, 61, 96, 120, 134,
139, 145, 146–147, 166, 189

Gabriola Island, 106–107, *111*,
206
Galiano Island, 87, 100–101, *104*
Galloping Goose Trail, 34–35, 50
Gardner, William, 205
Garrard, Frank and family,
167–168
Gaudin, James, 62, 68, 96, 102, 119,
147
Georgeson, Henry "Scotty"
and family, 82–83, 86, 89–90,
103

Gillespie, W.J., 97
Gold River, 172, 178, 179, *183*
Graham, Donald, 12, 84, 134
Greenall, Tony, 111
Gulf Islands National Park
Reserve, 89, 94, 99
Gurney, Arthur, 115–117, 186

Heanski, James, 94, 99
Helliwell Provincial Park, 124,
129
Hesquiat Peninsula Provincial
Park, 171, 174, *177*
hiking, 137, 151, 200
Holland family, 170
Hollyoak, Paul, 196
Hornby Island, 124, *129*
Humchitt, Harvey and family, 205

Jaksa, Chris, 12
Jensen, Jens, 176

Kains Island, 192–193, *197*
kayak or boat tours, 57, 65, 72, 93,
106, 112, 124
Kerrigan-Bruton, Sharon, 39–40,
41
Kidder, Ed and Pat, 184

Lally, Robert and family, 173–174,
186
lamp and reflector systems:
brightness scale, 24, 208; bulls-
eye lens, 24, 206; catoptric,
103, 208; dioptric, 96, 103, 109,
208; flashing of, 207, 209; lens
systems, 21–24, 208;
rotation, 25, 37, 148
lamps: acetylene, 24, 206; oil, 209;
wicks, 20, 22, 26
Lavoisier, Antoine, 23
lead poisoning, 40–41
Lennard Island, 164–170

light keepers: duties, 26–29, 40,
  142; hardships, 13–17; health
  issues, 40–41, 182; importance
  of, 64, 111; isolation of, 14, 16,
  148; and schooling, 116, 128,
  170; supplies, 201, 205; wages,
  30
lighthouse preservation, 10–11,
  84, 184
lighthouses: accessibility chart,
  11;
  de-staffing of, 38, 64; GPS
  co-ordinates list, 210; history
  of, 19–24; light lists, 208; map
  of, *31*; role of, 17–18
lightships, 16, 208
line of position (LOP), 21
Livermore, John, 58–59
logbooks, 28, 90, 173

Mäkelä, August, 190–191
Malcolm Island, 185–186, 188, *190*
Maliszewski, Todd and family,
  205
Mayne Island, 85–89, *91*
McDonough, Doug, 127
McNab, Thomas and family,
  168–169
mercury: baths, 37, 148, 209;
  poisoning, 41
Morrisey, W.E., 110
Morrison, Tom, 62

Nanaimo, 106, 107, 108, *111*
Nelson, Nels and family, 193,
  195
Nootka, 178–184
North Coast Trail, 200

Oak Bay, 57, *63*, 65, 72–73, 74
O'Kell, Harold Shorrock and
  family, 61–62

Pachena Point, 137, 144–150, 180
Pass of Melfort, 143, 159–160, 163,
  167–168
Paterson, Tom and family, 157
Pemberton, Joseph, 43, 44–45,
  46
petroglyphs, 106–107, 129–130,
  132
Piercy, Tom and family, 125, 127
Porlier Pass, 100–105, 209
Port Hardy, 200
Port McNeill, 185, *190*
Portlock Point, 93–99
Prevost Island, 93–96, *98*
Pulteney Point, 185–191

Quadra Island, 131–134, *135*
Quatsino, 192–198

Race Point, 100–105
Race Rocks, 42–49, 52
range lights, 102, 105, 127, 209
Redford, Edward, 173
Richardson, John and family, 97,
  148
Ritchie, Andrew and family, 48
Robertson II (schooner), 79–80
Routcliffe, Fred, 163
Royal Canadian Navy, 48, 112,
  173
Royal Navy, 46, 51, 52, 59–60, 95,
  161, 187
Royal Roads University, 35, 50
Ruckle Provincial Park, 93

Sadler, James and family, 30, 193,
  195–196
Salt Spring Island, 93, *104*
Saturna Island, 78–81, *83*, 84,
  126
Sheringham Point, 15, 33–41
Sheringham Point Lighthouse
  Preservation Society, 11, 33

ship wrecks, 60, 67, 90, 91–92;
   SS *Alpha*, 127; BC Ferries, 18,
   91–92; lists, 47–48, 143, 146;
   Pass of Melfort, 143, 159–160,
   163; *Robertson II*, 79–80;
   Uzbekistan, 146, 150; SS
   Valencia, 36, 145, 180
ships, navigation, 17–18, 21
Shirley, 33, 34, 35, *40*
Sisters Islets, 118–123, 126
Smith, Herbert, 136, 182
Sointula, 185, 186, 190–191
Sooke, 33, 35
Stevenson, Robert Louis, 25–26
Swanson, Art and family, 75–76

Tanod, Lynn, 12, 117
technology, 17–18, 205
Tofino, 158, 164–165, *169*, 172
Trial Islands, 57–64

MV *Uchuck III*, 178, 179, 184
Ucluelet, 158, 160–161, *162*
Uzbekistan, 146, 150

SS *Valencia*, 36, 145, 180
Vancouver Island, *81*
vega lights, 209
Victoria, 50, 57, 72
Virago Point, 100–105, 209

Warren, Sydney and family, *196*
Watson, George, 97–99
Wells, Richard, 150
West Coast Trail, 137–138,
   144–145, 148, *149*, 150
Westmoreland, Robert, 154
Winter Harbour, 192, 194, *197*
Wood, Rita and Richard, 117

Yuquot, 178–179, 181, 182

ABOUT THE AUTHORS

PETER JOHNSON was the "writer part of the team" for *To the Lighthouse*. He has published three previous books on late-nineteenth-century BC coastal history: *Glyphs and Gallows*, *Voyages of Hope*, and the award-winning *Quarantined: Life and Death at William Head Station, 1872–1959*. Once an avid sailor on the south coast, Peter is now into environmentally friendly cycle-touring. He lives in Vancouver.

JOHN WALLS was the project manager of the *To the Lighthouse* team. He is a director of the Sheringham Point Lighthouse Preservation Society. He was the primary photographer of Danda Humphreys's *Government Street* and is the author of and photographer for *Celebrating Victoria*. John is a kayaking aficionado and lives in beautiful Shirley, BC.

RICHARD PADDLE's partner, Sharon Kerrigan-Bruton, is the daughter of a British Columbia lighthouse keeper, and he has had a passion for lighthouses ever since they got together. He has travelled to almost every lighthouse in this province by charter boat, seaplane, and helicopter, amassing a rare collection of lighthouse photography. He wishes to thank the many light keepers and staff for their support and hospitality. Richard's photographs have been published in many brochures. He lives in Colwood, BC.